UNDERSTANDING BAKING

JOSEPH AMENDOLA
DONALD E. LUNDBERG

Jule Wilkinson
Book Editor

Tony Pronoitis
Art Director

Wilma Inman
Book Design

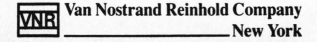 Van Nostrand Reinhold Company
——————————— New York

TABLE OF CONTENTS

Sixteenth Printing

FOREWORD

Bread is the most widely eaten food in the western world today and has been a staple food over the centuries. A painting on one of the walls of an Egyptian pyramid shows men kneading dough by trampling in it with their feet while maintaining their balance with the aid of a stick. Ancient Greece understood the art of puff pastry. Public bake shops appeared in ancient Rome even before the time of Christ

During the Middle Ages dining, like so many of the arts of fine living, became quite simple. At that time food was served on a trencher, and the trencher was a piece of thick bread placed on the plate. Other foods were piled upon it and the trencher soaked up the fats and juices from the various meats, poultries, and game placed on the trencher. The trencher was eaten last.

With the Renaissance, the Italians in the northern city states again developed keen interest in food. In the 16th century, Catherine de Medici was married to the Crown Prince of France, the Dauphin, (later Henry II) and brought with her to Paris a brigade of chefs and bakers. Catherine is credited with stimulating the French to take an interest in finer food preparation. Her bakers brought with them the recipes and skills for baking such items as cream custards, eclairs, tarts, macaroons, and cream puffs.

A school of baking was opened in Paris in 1780. About the same time, pastry baking became a specialized art and the pastry bakers set themselves up in business apart from the bread bakers.

In this country, wheat flour was at a premium during the Colonial period since wheat did not grow well in New England or along the eastern seaboard. Corn was the staple food of the colonial settlers. By the time of the American Revolution, bread again was an important part of the diet and Christopher Ludwig, as superintendent of the bakeries for the Continental Army, did much for the morale of the troops. George Washington grew wheat at Mt. Vernon and found milling an honorable profession. Mt. Vernon flour was famous for its high quality.

As settlers moved into the Middle West and wheat was grown over large areas, white flour became available to nearly everyone. The leavening agent for the bread made at the time came from several sources: the simplest was the fermentation of bacteria and wild yeast that could be made to grow in dough. A cowboy cook made his starter by mixing flour and potato water in a keg and leaving it in the sun to ferment. He often took it to bed with him to keep it warm through the long, cold nights.

3

#2   Another starter involved cornmeal, water, and sugar which was allowed to ferment over night. This was blended with flour, salt and other ingredients to yield "salt rising" or "sour dough" bread. Commercial yeast, a by-product of the brewing industry, became available in 1868.

#3   Another leavening agent much used in the 19th century was baking soda. It combined quickly with the lactic acid in sour milk or butter milk to release carbon dioxide which helped expand and raise the product. If a recipe called for sweet milk, cream of tartar could be added to get the chemical reaction going. Baking powder, a combination of baking soda and an acid, came along in 1856 and served the same purpose. All that was needed to start the reaction was to add water, salt and heat. Baking powder and commercially available yeast were great steps forward in the history of baking.

Much of history can be traced in the movement of a baked item from country to country. The croissant or crescent roll dates from the year 1686 when it was created in Budapest. The Ottoman Turks were besieging the city and had tunneled under the city walls into the heart of the city. Bakers who worked during the night heard the sounds of the Turks digging and gave the alarm. To reward the bakers who had saved the city, the privilege of making a crescent roll was granted to them since the crescent was the emblem which decorated the Turkish flag. The croissant is widely popular as a breakfast item in France today.

Strudel, the marvelous paper-thin dough product, had a similar history. Apparently thin layered dough was first used in the Near East to make baklava. Baklava is made up of paper-thin sheets of dough piled in layers and filled with honey and nuts. This dessert moved westward with the Turks as they came into Hungary. Later it was carried from Hungary into Germany and Austria when Hungary became a part of the Austro-Hungarian Empire.

The move to convenience in the bake shop came about the turn of the century. Self-rising flour that contained baking powder was available prior to 1900. Pancake flour was developed during World War I. By the early thirties a biscuit mix became available to the housewife and doughnut mixes began being used by the baker. The first cake mix, that for gingerbread, was sold in the mid thirties. Soon after, pie crust mixes and corn muffin mixes appeared.

Cake mixes were marketed before World War II but during that war there was a shortage of sugar and shortening. Cake mixes which included these items did not require ration points. Many housewives were at work in industry and the mixes were popular. Today few home baked cakes are made from "scratch". Only eggs and water are added to most cake mixes now bought in the store.

The first cakes in this country were pound cakes, so called because they contained one pound of butter, one pound of flour, one pound of eggs and one pound of sugar. Sponge cakes were also possible to make without the use of baking soda or baking powder. Cakes as we know them today were not possible until the invention of baking powder when a cake could be leavened and built up in layers. The angel cake is an exception since it is leavened completely by the hot air and steam initially made available by whipping and "folding in" egg whites

A big step forward in the making of cakes came in the 1930's when emulsifiers were added to shortening. These new shortenings, called "High-Ratio shortenings", made it possible for the batter to carry greater proportions of shortening, sugar, milk, and eggs to flour. Once the high ratio shortenings were available it was not long before flours were introduced to accommodate them. These flours were ground more finely and permitted greater absorption and a finer crumb in the cake. Today pre-mixes are widely used in institutional and commercial food service kitchens. Professional bakers, too, are turning to them. It is likely that bake shops will be using pre-mixes almost exclusively in the near future.

Mechanized equipment in the bake shop has changed baking from a job demanding long hours and hard work to something approaching an industrial process. Much of the job of baking has been de-skilled. The job is broken down into its separate parts with most of the work done by machinery, each man doing only one small part of the total process. The small bake shop manned by two or three persons is doomed to disappear unless the use of pre-mixes is adopted. Large industrial plants produce most of the bread. In such plants only a few persons direct and control the whole establishment. Most of the employees are machine operators; only a few employees perform the few specialized tasks.

This change to mechanization has given the professional baker a new importance and demanded from him knowledge and technical skills not previously required. He becomes a technician as well as a craftsman. In addition to being able to roll and shape doughs he must understand something about the ingredients used and at least a little about the physics and chemistry of baking. The purpose of this book is to provide that simple and elementary understanding.

INTRODUCTION

heat

1. What is Baking? The application of heat to food in an "oven". More exactly, as used in this book, baking refers to the application of heat to doughs, batters, and certain dessert mixtures. To bake food, _____ is applied to certain mixtures in an oven.

oven

2. By definition, baked products are those items produced in a bakeshop. They include breads, rolls, cakes, pies, and other pastries. They also may include a number of baked desserts such as puddings and meringues. When we think of baked products we usually think of products which include a large percentage of wheat flour and that are cooked in an _____ .

flour and water

3. Doughs and batters are usually mixtures of wheat flour and water to which salt is added. Milk, eggs, sugar, shortening, flavorings and a leavening agent are often added. The ingredients most common to baked products are _____ .

4. Each common ingredient in a baked product adds a particular character and performs a particular function in producing the finished product. Listed below in tabulated form are the various functions performed by each ingredient.

1. Functions	2. Flour	3. Sugar	4. Shortening	5. Eggs	6. Leavening	7. Water
1. Structure Builder (Toughener)	X			X *(coagulation)*		
2. Bulk Builder	X	X				
3. Dryer	X	X		X		
4. Tenderizer		X	X		X	
5. Moistener		X	X	X		X
6. Flavor (including sweetening)		X	X *(butter)*	X		
7. Color Builder		X		X		
8. Lubricant			X			
9. Creaming Agent		X	X			
10. Binding Agent				X		
11. Lightening Agent				X	X	

sponge cake - air incorporation.

strength

5. From the chart we see that flour acts to dry the product, provide bulk and add _____.

tenderizer

6. Sugar is a tenderizer/toughener.

toughener

7. Eggs are a tenderizer/toughener.

Flour and liquid mixtures can be classified according to proportion of liquid added to the flour.

	Liquid	Flour	Consistency	Product Examples
Pour batters	One Part	One Part	Pours in a steady stream	Popover, Griddle Cakes
Drop batters	One Part	Two Parts	Forms large drops when poured	Muffins and Fritters
Soft doughs	One Part	Three Parts	Sticky to touch	Bread, Biscuits, Yeast Rolls
Stiff doughs	One Part	Four Parts	Firm to touch	Pie Crusts, Cookies, Noodles

soft

8. Bread dough would be classified as _____.

drop batte

9. A muffin mixture is classified as a <u>drop batter</u>/<u>soft</u> dough.

stiff

10. A pie crust is an example of a _____ dough.

pour batter

11. A popover mixture would be an example of a_____.

soft dough

12. Some mixtures are classed as pastes, somewhere between a soft dough and a batter in consistency. Examples are eclair paste and puff paste. Eclair paste, also known as choux paste, is made by cooking flour, shortening and water. The batter is cooled to 150°F. and eggs added. The end product is a smooth, velvety paste, thick enough to retain its shape when placed in a pan.

Pastes can be shaped by forcing them out of a pastry tube. Paste has a consistency somewhat less than that of_____.

Eggs and
shortening

13. What ingredients added to a dough tend to make the dough into a paste?

pastes

14. Flour and liquid mixtures can be classed as batters, dough and _____.

True

15. What is preferred in a baked item is largely a matter of food habit, what the eater has learned to like. In this country, white bread, for example, with a fine even crumb and large volume is most popular. Many people, however, like a tough, chewy crust like that found in Italian or French bread. Others like a coarse loaf with some bran included in the flour. Cakes with a high proportion of sugar and eggs and a tender texture are most popular.

In speaking of quality of a baked item, we must always relate the term to whatever the eater expects in the product.

True or False: Baking standards and formulas must be in terms of what the eater expects or wants.

Probably not.
Rather, he
should make
the item
which is
most pleasing
to his
customers.

16. To make the product desired, the baker has a wide range of ingredients and formulas to choose from.

True or False: He should choose those formulas which produce a product which he personally likes best.

17. The baker has a choice of flours to use and if he is to get the final product he wants, he must understand what each flour will do to the product. Flours are usually classified as cake, pastry, all purpose, and bread. Most home kitchens use an all purpose flour which is somewhere in between a pastry and a bread flour in its characteristics. To get optimum results, however, the baker must use a flour that is right for the product he wants to produce. For example, the protein content of flour for use in an angel food cake should be lower than that used in a loaf cake, and both would be lower in protein than flour used for making a pie crust.

True or False: The baker must understand the differences in various flours and their effects upon the final product.

18. Fats used in most baking are known as shortening. They are used for reasons other than the fact that most people like the taste of fats. Shortening surrounds gluten in dough, makes it less continuous, and the product more tender.

When a batter or dough is baked, the fat globules entrap gas and expand.

Shortening has a "lubricating" effect on doughs that makes them easy to chew and to swallow.

It is reasonable to expect the baker to know something about the fats he uses and what effects they have on the finished baked item.

More fat

19. Pastry includes a wide variety of products made from doughs containing medium to large amounts of fats. Sweet rolls, for example, contain a medium amount of fat and are leavened with yeast. Danish or other rolled-in sweet doughs have butter, margarine or shortening spread between layers of dough and puff paste contains so much fat that a portion of it is also folded or laid into the dough. Pie crust contains 40 to 75% as much shortening as flour.

Pastry doughs are identified by the fact that they contain more/less fat (shortening) than other doughs.

3 pounds

20. The bakers have developed for themselves a unique system for calculating formulas for all types of baked products which is simple, effective, yet uninvolved. Instead of formulating on the basis of true percentages that in each case must add up to 100%, he does so on the basis of so many pounds of any ingredient involved to 100 pounds of flour, (the baker's basic ingredient). If he uses 2 pounds of eggs to 10 pounds of flour, he is using 20% of eggs. If 12 pounds of sugar are used to 10 pounds of flour, it is 120% sugar.

This system is known as baker's percentages. It simplifies formula variation because it provides a simple means of varying one ingredient at a time without having to recalculate the percentage relationship of the other ingredients to this change.

Suppose a formula calls for 30% shortening and 10 pounds of flour are used. How many pounds of eggs are needed?

4 pounds
(20% of 20 lbs.)

21. If a formula calls for 20 pounds of flour and 20% sugar, how many pounds of sugar are needed?

REVIEW

1. What kind of dough—soft or stiff—is called for in these products
   Bread _____
   Cookies _____
   Biscuits _____
   Pie Crust _____

2. In bakery formulas each ingredient used is expressed as a percentage of the _____ used.

3. Suppose a formula called for 110% sugar and 50 pounds of flour. How much sugar would be included?

4. The bakery usually stocks three kinds of flour—bread, pastry and cake. Where does all-purpose fit in?

5. The common ingredients in a baked product are flour, sugar, shortening, eggs, leavening and water.

   Which of these ingredients act to tenderize the product?

6. Which of the common ingredients used in baking acts as a "lubricant"?

7. Which two ingredients are known as creaming agents?

8. Which items are drying agents?

9. Which are tenderizers?

10. Give two examples of products made from the stiff doughs.

11. Sweet roll dough would be an example of what type of dough, soft or stiff?

12. What type of dough is a muffin made from?

13. Griddle cakes would be an example of <u>pour</u>/<u>drop</u> batter

14. True or False: The best type of bread is tnat which is liked by the customer.

15 What type of flour would you likely find in the usual home: all purpose pastry or bread?

16 Most of the fat which is usea in baking is known as _____ __.

The Baking Process

crust

1   The baking process takes place in an oven as heat is applied to doughs or batters   The process can be broken down into these steps:

A.   Gases are formed and expand

B.   The gluten and eggs present are stretched to form a new structure   These become firm (coagulate) and provide chewiness in the product. They both are tougheners.

C.   The starches present take on moisture and become firm (gelatinize).

D.   Some of the water evaporates.

E.   Shortenings present melt and release air bubbles that in the case of batters help to leaven the batter. The oil (melted shortening) then deposits around cell walls and makes them less tough.

F.   Flavors develop and brown colors appear because of the caramelization of sugar and browning of the milk, gluten and egg proteins.

G.   A crust forms as water is driven off by the heat, a process that occurs first on the surface. The baking process involves heat, gas formation, coagulation of proteins, gelatinization of starches, vaporization of water, melting of shortening, development of flavors and color and the formation of a _____.

The gases that are formed. These include steam, hot air, carbon dioxide, depending on what leavening agent is used.

2. During the baking process, what is it that raises the dough or batter to create a new and large form which is of lighter density than the dough or batter?

The gluten and eggs present.

3. What ingredients are mainly responsible for giving a dough product its chewiness or toughness?

gelatinization

4. When a starch is heated in the presence of moisture and expands (swells), then becomes firm, this is known as _____.

The shortenings or oils present. Sugar also acts as a tenderizing agent.

5. What is it that tenderizes a dough or batter product?

gas

6. Let's look at the baking process step by step. First the gas formation and the leavening action.

Depending upon the leavening agent used in baking, gases formed are hot air and steam, carbon dioxide and, when baking ammonia is used, ammonia bicarbonate. Some items such as eclairs, pound cake, angel cake etc. are leavened by hot air and steam only.

Most cakes are leavened by the carbon dioxide gas formed from baking powder. A few products are leavened by baking soda and an acid as in some cookies (or chocolate cakes).

Leavening of a baked product involves the expansion of a _____.

Carbon dioxide gas

7. Baked dough products rise or are leavened by the action of a gas—usually carbon dioxide—which expands the dough. CO_2 is formed by the action of yeast which breaks down sugar to CO_2 and alcohol and by the action of an acid or heat on soda which releases CO_2. Baking powders contain soda plus an acid ingredient that reacts with the soda when moistened and the product is heated. Double action baking powders are called this because they release from a fifth to a third of their gas while at room temperature when moistened. The remainder of the gas is given off during the baking process; hence the baking powder acts twice and its name, "double-acting". A single acting baking powder will give all of its gas in the cold stage when moistened. This makes it difficult to handle in quantity baking.

will it work best as well if put into oven and not allowed to remain at room temp.

What gas is responsible for most of the leavening action in baked dough products?

During the baking when heat is applied.

8. Double acting baking powders give off CO_2 twice—when first mixed into a product and at what other time?

Carbon dioxide

9. In using soda alone as a leavening agent we may add an acid such as sour milk, molasses or buttermilk. Soda that develops carbon dioxide alone in a product without an acid ingredient to react with it (by heat alone) may leave a soapy flavor in the baked product. Sometimes we add an excess of soda to a chocolate cake so an alkaline action is developed and this causes the chocolate to turn a nice reddish color. However, we do this at the expense of the flavor for we may get this soapy flavor in such a cake.

Baking soda and acid produce leavening by the formation of what gas?

Most of the gas escapes; and when the shells are opened so that the fillings can be inserted, any gas that is left escapes.

10. Still another leavening agent used, but not widely, is baking ammonia (ammonium bicarbonate). In the presence of moisture and heat, baking ammonia changes to carbon dioxide and ammonia gas. It is used in making cookies and choux pastry (for making the shells of cream puffs, eclairs and the small cream puffs known as profiteroles). Ammonia does not discolor the dough as would baking soda. The word choux means cabbage in French; the choux pastry probably takes its name from the fact that some of the pastries look like little cabbages.

Would you think that in using ammonia as a leavening agent the residual gas would be dangerous?

Flour containing gluten

11. To achieve a leavened product, we need (a) a gas acting on the dough, paste or batter and (b) the presence of what substance in the dough that stretches and forms the structure for the raised product?

Gluten or egg protein because they alone will stretch under the pressure of the expanding gas.

12. In the leavening action the gas, whatever it is, expands into cells already in the dough or batter, (by creaming or mixing) stretching and enlarging them. The cell walls that are expanded are made up of gluten and starch.

Which ingredients in a baked product are absolutely essential if the product is to rise?

The gas which is released from the baking powder or soda expands with heat, stretching the gluten which coagulates and firms, giving the biscuit its shape and texture.

13. Carbon dioxide performs what task in a baking powder biscuit?

No, air and steam also act to expand the dough.

14. Steam and hot air are other gases that also expand dough. When water changes to steam, its volume increases 1600 times. This accounts for almost all of the leavening action in the baking of popovers, cream puff shells, crackers, and in pie crust.

Is it necessary for carbon dioxide gas to be present for a dough to rise?

yeast

15. Yeast is used to make bread and sweet dough rise. Yeast action begins during the time the dough is allowed to ferment and ends in the oven when the internal temperature of the dough reaches around 140°F.

Ethyl alcohol is produced by the action of the yeast on some of the sugars in the dough. The yeast also releases carbon dioxide. The carbon dioxide is the main leavening agent in a yeast dough, although gases from water (steam) and ethyl alcohol may help some in the leavening.

Carbon dioxide gas is formed by the action of baking soda, baking powder and what other common baking ingredient?

fermented

16. Yeast is also used to leaven such items as Baba au rum, English muffins and crumpets. Sour dough and old fashioned hot cake batter is "started" by use of an old dough or battei in which fermentation is quite complete. Such a "starter" is highly acid or sour—hence the name "sour dough". The 49'ers of Alaska carried bits of this dough in their pockets, keeping the yeast oi bacteria alive to be used at their next campsite.

A sourdough refers to an individual who uses sourdough as his yeast product, but it also refers to the dough that has been well_____.

Not quite. The yeast gives off an enzyme, zy- mase, that splits some sugars into alcohol and carbon dioxide

17. The leavening action of yeast is most interesting. Gases are formed in the process known as <u>fermentation.</u> The fermentation we are talking about is the splitting of sugar by the action of yeast enzymes to form carbon dioxide and alcohol. The ancient Egyptians knew about the leavening action of yeast but did not understand what was taking place.

True or False: Yeast as it grows gives off the carbon dioxide that raises the dough.

CO_2

18. During fermentation enzymes in the yeast known as zymase change the sugars, dextrose and levulose into carbon dioxide and ethyl alcohol:

$$C_6 H_{12} O_6 + yeast\ 2\ CO_2 + 2C_2H_5OH$$

Dextrose or levulose	carbon dioxide	alcohol
100 parts	48.9 parts	51.1 parts

Temperatures of about 78° to 90^oF. are best for fermentation. Above 110^oF. yeast action is slowed and at about 138^oF. yeast is destroyed.

Enzymes in the yeast act on simple sugars to produce_____and alcohol which causes the dough to rise. This is the fermentation process.

same as

19. Yeast is in the air practically everywhere. Saccharomyces cerevisiae is the yeast that is responsible for splitting sugar into carbon dioxide and alcohol and is the yeast wanted for fermenting dough products. In fact, the name of the yeast—saccharomyces, means "sugar splitter".

Commercial baker's yeast is purchased as compressed yeast or active dry yeast. Compressed yeast can be bought in one or five pound blocks. If refrigerated, it keeps its fermentation power up to 4 to 5 weeks. If frozen, it can be stored for months. Compressed yeast is about 70% water.

If most of the water is taken out of compressed yeast we have active dry yeast.

Bakers' yeast can be bought in compressed or dry form. The dried form is the same as/different from the compressed form with the water removed.

When the heat approaches 138°F. the yeast dies.

20. Dry yeast can be used interchangeably with compressed yeast. Only 40% as much of the dry yeast is needed.

Compressed yeast should be stored between 30 and 45 degrees Fahrenheit. Dry yeast can be stored at room temperature. When the temperature rises and moisture is present the yeast comes to life and begins to grow.

Yeast action varies with the temperature:

60°-70°F.	Slow reaction
80°F.	Normal reaction
90°-100°F.	Fast reaction
138°F.	Yeast dies

Looking at the chart what do you think happens to yeast during the baking process?

Warm water
(In large
scale baking
yeast is
mixed directly
into the dough.)

21. In small-quantity baking, yeast is <u>conditioned</u> by being placed in warm water. Compressed yeast is sprinkled into water that is about 100°F. Dry active yeast is sifted into water at about 110°F. Both are allowed to stand about 3 minutes before stirring.

To get yeast ready for use in small-quantity baking, we <u>condition</u> it by placing it in_____.

Yes, a certain
amount of
minerals is
desirable for
tightening the
gluten. Soft
water lacks such
minerals. The
yeast food
makes up for
their absence.

22. Since yeast is a living one-cell plant, it needs food as does any other living plant or animal. Besides the food found in the flour and water, many bakers add <u>yeast foods</u> which cause the yeast to be more active and to give larger volume of a dough product. The yeast foods also reduce the time required for the dough to rise (proof). Yeast foods contain bromate, ammonium chloride and gypsum.

Since these are minerals, would a yeast food tend to offset the undesirable effects of using soft water?

flavor

23. Much of the characteristic aroma of bread and similar baked items comes directly from the activity of the yeast.

The yeast in bread, in addition to being the principal cause of the leavening action, also adds _____to the bread.

The browning
of the sugars,
milk and
proteins

24. The flavor of baked goods is developed from a variety of factors, among them being the sugar, fat and flavorings present. What baking action also adds flavor and some color?

coagulated
protein

25. When starch gelatinizes it helps give the baked product some firmness and most of its bulk.

Starch together with _____ gives the product its structure and bulk.

REVIEW

1. During the baking process dough is leavened (raised) by the action of expanding _____.

2. The gases press against the dough stretching _____ protein present.

3. The proteins present become firm and are largely responsible for the structure of the product. Gluten and eggs are considered <u>tougheners/tenderizers.</u>

4. Name two tenderizers _____ and _____.

5. Where does the carbon dioxide that is made available by the fermentation process come from?

6. Yeast used in baking is <u>dead/living.</u>

7. At what temperature is yeast killed?

8. The best temperature for fermentation which takes place before baking is about _____.

9. Yeast foods make the yeast <u>more/less</u> active.

10. If yeast activity is speeded, proof time (fermentation time) is <u>longer/shorter.</u>

11. True or False: Soft water is best for proper gluten development.

12. Eclairs are leavened by what gases?

13. The technical term for the process which takes place when starches are cooked is _____.

14. When acted upon by a yeast enzyme, zymase, sugar splits into _____ and _____.

The Magic of Gluten

gluten

1. Mix flour and water together and knead. Lo and behold, it begins to become stretchy and elastic. The proteins in the flour take up the water (hydrate). <u>Gluten</u> is being developed. The proteins and water form a molecular network that can be stretched. When heated to about 165°F. it becomes firm and provides the structural framework of the baked dough product.

What is the ingredient that permits doughs to enlarge and take on a new shape when baked?

water

2. Mixing flour and water to form a dough is something like mixing sand, cement and water to form concrete. Protein in the flour resembles the cement; starch in a flour is like sand.

Adding water to the flour and mixing develops the gluten to give strength to the dough, just as adding water and sand to cement and mixing sets off a chemical reaction which gives strength to the sand and cement.

The water must be mixed with the flour so that the gluten strands can develop. Try forming a pie dough using only fat and flour. When baked the crust would have no strength and crumble.

To form an elastic dough with strength, the flour must be mixed with _____ .

developed

3. As wheat flour and water are kneaded, gluten is _____ .

Protein

4. Not all of the protein in flour will form gluten but that which does is the part that enables the dough or batter to stretch and rise. Proteins in flour vary in the amount and quality of gluten that is developed. Flour is said to be strong or weak according to the amount and toughness or elasticity of the gluten formed.

What ingredient in flour largely determines the strength of the flour?

strength

5. A dough's elasticity or stretch is related to the _____ of the flour used.

Protein

6. Strength of the flour is dependent primarily, but not entirely, on the amount and type of protein present in the flour.

Gluten strength depends mostly upon the wheat variety, the kind of wheat, but also upon the growing conditions and the storage conditions. For bread and rolls we need a strong flour but strength is not necessarily an asset. Cakes, for example, should be made with weak flour, pastries with a flour of intermediate strength.

Strength of the flour is most closely related to what constituent in the flour?

Small

7. The amount of gluten present in flour is related to the amount of protein in the flour. Wheat flour ranges in protein content from about 6.5 to 15 percent. If a baked item is to rise and assume a new enlarged form, some gluten must be present so that the dough will stretch and harden when in the expanded form.

The amount of gluten needed for a product varies considerably. Bread, eclairs and pound cake may contain large amounts of gluten to give the desired structure, while cake, cookies and some pastries require much less because fewer structure-building properties are desired. In a product such as pie dough low gluten is wanted so that the crust will have a "sharp break" (break easily).

Cakes and cookies need comparatively large/small amounts of gluten development.

8. Much of baking knowledge is concerned with the amount, nature and control of the gluten which is developed in a particular flour.

Breads baked on the hearth (on stones and not in pans) require high protein flour that when baked will be strong enough not to flatten under the weight of the dough and to withstand the strong leavening action of the large amount of carbon dioxide gas developed by the yeast.

Cake flour, on the other hand, must be made from a soft wheat (low protein content). If bread flour were used, the cake would be tough. You can make a cake with bread flour if you increase the fat, but the product is never as good as when cake flour is used.

Flours in a middle range between those needed for cakes and cookies are necessary for pastries and hot breads such as rolls, biscuits and muffins.

The protein content and gluten development of flour that is best for pastries and hot breads are more/less than those contained in bread flours.

9. Muffins are characteristically light and fluffy and the problem in making them is to avoid developing the gluten in the flour. Mix the batter as little as possible. Even during the process of putting the batter into a pan too much manipulation causes a tough muffin. In a baking powder biscuit dough we want a stronger structure and so we will work the dough more than a muffin batter. However, too much kneading or working will destroy quality in the biscuit.

If we mix biscuit dough too much we will get what?

10. For Danish and sweet rolls, bread flour can be used but some formulas call for the addition of some pastry flour. Why?

Wheat

11. Only wheat flour can be kneaded to develop gluten to any extent. Rye flour contains enough protein to do so but other substances present do not permit gluten development. To develop gluten we need what kind of flour?

Strong, be-
cause the
dough must
stretch a great
deal to form
a large loaf.

12. The variety of wheat, the growing conditions and the soil produce wheats of different hardness and softness. Hard wheat produces strong flours. From strong flours gluten can be developed that stretches farther before tearing. Taking a guess, what kind of flour, strong or weak, would you use for bread?

Weak. The
thing we prize
about cakes is
their tenderness.
Weak flours
make for tender
cakes.

13. Again, thinking about strength, what kind of flour would be used for a cake?

weak

14. Soft wheat produces weak flours. Hard wheats result in flours that are strong. While we speak of the strength of a flour, the wheat it is made from is spoken of as being hard or soft. Soft wheat produces a _____ flour.

strong

15. Hard wheat results in a _____ flour.

protein

16. Other factors than the amount of protein affect the quality of the flour. These are not well understood. The principal factor in a wheat and flour that determines the baking characteristic is the amount of _____ in the wheat.

No, if all the gluten is developed the biscuit would be chewy like bread. Most of us like tender biscuits.

17. As flour is worked (kneaded) by hand or by mixing machine, the dough becomes elastic. The amount of kneading or mixing determines how much gluten is developed.

In some products, like bread, we want maximum gluten development. For tender biscuits, would you want maximum gluten development?

Quite easily. The gluten is broken down and the dough loses its ability to expand.

18. Gluten is not like rubber or gum that springs back after many stretchings. Stretch dough too much and the gluten strands break.

Can we overmix a dough?

gluten

19. Much of the skill of baking centers around the control of gluten development. The more protein present and the more gluten developed, the more chewy will be the product. Hearth baked breads, those that are not panned (baked in a pan), require maximum gluten to support the loaf. Cake which is supposed to be light and tender requires minimum gluten. Flaky crust pastry calls for some (only) gluten development.

The substance which provides a frame and is the principal support for baked goods is _____.

Less. The bran apparently cuts the gluten strands and has a diluting effect on the protein. The loaf will be smaller.

20. Suppose we use whole wheat flour—that containing the bran and the germ as the endosperm. Would we get more or less gluten development than with white flour?

21. Gluten is strengthened by the presence of most minerals. Water contains minerals and the so-called dough improvers contain minerals which act to strengthen gluten.

strengthens

The presence of minerals strengthens/weakens gluten.

22. The amount of water absorbed by a dough largely depends on the amount of protein or gluten present. The more protein, the greater the amount of water required to make up the dough. Starch present absorbs comparatively little water.

Bread dough because of its higher protein content.

Which dough would take more water: bread dough or pastry dough?

23. The amount of water absorbed by the dough is a guide to the amount of protein present. Which dough would take up more water, cookie dough or pastry dough?

Pastry dough since it is likely to contain more protein.

24. Knowing that fat (shortening) surrounds gluten strands, do you think that adding shortening to a dough would help or hinder the development of gluten?

It hinders the development since it makes the gluten strands less continuous. Fat is a tenderizer. So too is sugar.

True

25. As gluten is <u>developed</u> in a dough it takes up water and becomes stretchable.

To roll into pie dough, strudel dough and Danish pastry dough, the gluten stretches into longer and longer strands. After gluten is stretched it tends to shorten up, to partially retain its original length. A dough that is rolled out then handles much better if it is allowed to <u>relax.</u>

True or False: When gluten is stretched as a dough is rolled out, the gluten strands tend to partially shorten up.

The gluten strands

26. To allow the gluten to adjust to its new length after being stretched, a dough is <u>relaxed.</u> In pie dough the dough must be <u>relaxed</u> overnight. With Danish pastry the dough is usually relaxed for 30 minutes or more between each rolling. During the period of relaxation the starch takes up some of the water and the gluten strands are given time to adjust to their new longer length.

We relax dough primarily so that it will roll out more easily and take on a new and flatter form. What part of the dough are we most concerned with in the relaxing period?

Yes, by over-mixing the dough some of the gluten strands are broken. The dough begins to resemble that made with pastry flour. Not a recommended practice because bread flour is usually more costly. Over-mixing is also costly in time and power.

27. Ordinarily pie dough is made using pastry flour. Pastry flour contains less protein than bread flour, more than cake flour. Is it possible to use bread flour for making pie crusts?

minerals, fat,
overmixing

28. Gluten is strengthened by the presence of___
_____, weakened by the presence of_____
or by_____.

relaxed

29. To stretch a dough it is rolled out. Usually, to allow the gluten to adjust to the new length of the strands, it is _____ for a period of time.

wheat flour

30. The amount of gluten developed in a dough depends primarily on the kind of _____ used.

minimum gluten development

31. In some products we want maximum gluten development; in others, minimum gluten development. How about angel food cakes?

1. The kind and amount of protein in the flour relates to the type of gluten that can be developed from it. If the flour will produce a large amount of elastic gluten, it would be called a strong/weak flour.

2. For cakes we want a strong/weak flour?

3. For bread we would want a strong/weak flour?

4. In some products we want to develop the maximum gluten possible. Suppose we over-mix a dough, what happens to the gluten?

5. For tender biscuits we develop maximum/minimum gluten.

6. What effect do minerals have on the gluten?

7. Which dough will absorb more water, that with high protein or low protein?

8. To "relax" a dough, we allow it to stand and the gluten to _____ _____.

9. A relaxed dough is easier/more difficult to handle than a dough that is not relaxed.

10. Which contains more protein, cake or pastry flour?

Selecting the Right Flour

cake, pastry
and bread

1. Flours vary widely in the way they perform in baking. The baker selects a flour to produce a particular product. Or, he buys a mix, the flour of which has been carefully selected to produce the desired end product. Cake flours are for cakes. Pastry flours for pastry and bread flour for breads. All purpose flour is a compromise product, a mixture of the various flours, made to simplify the housewife's inventory and supposed to be able to produce any baked product in a creditable manner. The professional baker seldom uses all purpose flour because he wants the specific flour to produce a particular optimum product.

The professional baker is likely to stock what three flours?

endosperm

2. To understand the differences in flour, let's look at a kernel of wheat.

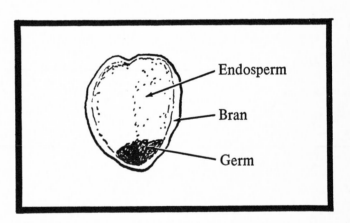

We see that the largest part of the wheat kernel is the _____.

bran

3. Around the outside of the kernel is the ____.

germ

4. Grind the entire kernel into flour and we have whole wheat flour. It is very difficult to keep "fresh" because it contains the germ which is about 11% fat. This fat turns rancid when exposed to oxygen due to the action of some enzymes naturally present in the wheat.

Whole wheat flour contains the endosperm, the bran, and the _____.

endosperm

5. White flour is made using only the endosperm. The kernel is broken up into a meal, then bolted (sifted). The bran is lifted off by air. The germ is separated off.

White flour is made up of what part of the wheat kernel?

fancy patent or
extra short
flour

6. About 72% of the wheat kernel comes out as flour. What's left is used for animal feed.

The finest flour is known as <u>fancy patent</u> or <u>extra short</u>.

Then come <u>short</u>, <u>medium</u>, and <u>patent</u> flours. Straight flour is a combination of the others.

The finest ground flour, most free of bran and germ, might be labeled a _____.

7. Next, let's look at the composition of wheat flour:

> Protein 6.5 - 15%
> Starch 68 - 76%
> Lipids (fat-like compounds) 1.5%
> Ash (minerals) .3 - 1%
> Fiber .4 - .5%
> Moisture 11 - 13%

Although the largest constituent of wheat flour is starch, it is the _____ which primarily affects its baking quality.

high

8. Rub some of the white flours found in the usual bake shop between your fingers. Some will be found to be gritty or <u>hard.</u> Others will be extremely powdery or <u>soft.</u>

The hardness or softness is related to the proportion of protein in starch in the flour. Starch grinds into a fine powder. Protein is broken into larger particles that can be felt when rubbed.

Rub a white flour between the fingers. If gritty it is likely to be <u>high/low</u> in protein.

The bread would rise very little and would be extremely heavy and dense.

9. Besides wheat flour, we have rye, graham and soy flour, potato, corn, and farina.

Although rye flour contains sufficient protein to develop gluten, gummy substances in the flour prevent gluten from developing. It is usually available in three grades of color: white, medium, and dark. Since rye flour does not form gluten, it is mixed with strong wheat flour, in varying proportions depending upon the type of rye bread wanted, such as American rye, sour rye, pumpernickel and sweet or pan rye.

What do you think would happen to the bread if no wheat flour were added to the rye flour?

10. Soy flour is more nutritious than any other flour. Although soy flour is highly nutritious, its flavor is not well accepted by North Americans. Up to 8% soy flour can be added to wheat flour if additional oxidizing agents such as potassium bromate are added. Rolls containing soy flour and oxidizing agents can be made superior to bread baked from wheat flour alone as measured by volume and fineness of grain.

Can you make bread from soy flour alone?

It would not
rise properly
because soy
flour does not
develop gluten
and Americans
would not eat
it because of
its flavor.

11. Soft wheat flour (low protein) is called for when making cookies, crackers, and pretzels. Soft wheat is also used in cakes, doughnuts, and other cake-like products.

True or False: Soft wheat flour is used for items that do not need strong gluten.

true

12. Graham flour is flour to which bran has been added but which is very finely ground. It was named after a miller of whole wheat who advocated its use.

Is Graham flour similar to whole wheat flour?

Yes, both contain bran but in the graham flour the bran is finely ground.

13. Suppose you have nothing but bread flour and would like to use it for making pastry or even some types of cake. Would it be possible to soften the flour by adding starch?

Yes, this is done at times

14. A flour made from durum wheat is especially high in protein and has its own yellow amber color and nutty flavor. It is used mostly for pasta products such as macaroni, spaghetti and noodles.

Would durum flour be desirable for French or Italian types of breads which require high protein content?

Yes, it is so used especially in France and Italy

15. FLOUR ADDITIVES AND MATURING A-GENTS

True: for some people who don't understand their purpose. But flour additives as allowed by law are good for the purposes intended.

Because wheats vary and their growing conditions vary, the resulting flours may not be exactly what is wanted. Flour is bleached to whiten it.

We may need to add enzymes to the flour so that fermentation can take place properly.

We may want to strengthen the gluten in the flour by adding oxygen to it.

We may want to increase the vitamins and iron content.

For these and other reasons some flours are bleached and certain additives are put into them.

Such additives improve the flour in various ways. An additive is something added to a food for a particular purpose. Flour additives aid the baker and the consumer.

True or False: An additive can be a "dirty" word.

Mature it by adding oxygen to it.

16. Bleached flour is flour that has had one of several bleaching agents added to it by the miller These agents whiten the flour by removing the yellow color (the carotenoids) present.

Some bleaching agents also mature or "age" the flour which means that oxygen is added to the flour and the gluten becomes stronger or more elastic.

White cakes are made with bleached flour because of the white color desired.

Cookies, pies and crackers are usually made with unbleached flour.

Some bleaching agents, besides whitening the flour, also _____ the flour.

17. Flour can be <u>matured</u> by letting it sit in storage. Gradually, the surrounding air combines with some of the flour. This is a slow and costly process and the oxygen does not reach the flour uniformly therefore the miller is likely to add a <u>maturing</u> agent to the flour which accomplishes the same purpose in a shorter time.

The most widely used <u>additive</u> for this purpose is <u>potassium bromate.</u> It is one of several gluten oxidizing agents which have the effect of making the gluten more elastic and stretchable.

<u>Bromated flour</u> would most likely be used for <u>bread/cake</u>.

18. Potassium bromate is added to flour by the miller, not the baker. Only a few parts per million are added. This amount is so small that it is no health hazard, and is less than what normally occurs in many seafoods.

Potassium bromate has no bleaching effect on the flour. It is inert until water is added. Because it makes the gluten more elastic and stretchable the dough is easier to handle. The fermented dough will stretch and hold gas better. The baked product is bigger.

Would you use bromated flour for cakes?

19. Not all flour is bromated; some flour does not need it. Other flours need a combination of maturing agents. Chlorine dioxide and bromate are sometimes added together.

The addition of <u>maturing agents</u> to flour is best done by whom, the baker or the miller?

20. The most widely used <u>maturing agent</u> added to flour is_____.

21. Potassium bromate does what to the gluten?

Bread; we need strong gluten for bread; a cake.

Probably not, because the bromated flour is not bleached.

The miller. The process is much too complicated to do in the bakeshop.

potassium bromate

Makes it more stretchable and elastic

22. Other additives are put in flour to accomplish particular purposes. Malted wheat or barley flour (from germinated grain) is added to flour that contains too few of the natural enzymes needed to convert starch into the sugars. The word "enzyme" comes from the Greek word "to leaven".

If there are too few of these enzymes, dough will fail to rise properly. Too many, and the dough is sticky, tends to run. The baked product may contain gummy spots.

Dough that is leavened by yeast must have enough enzymes present to provide sugars on which the yeast can act.

The reason malted wheat may be added to flour is to provide more of the right kind of _____.

enzymes

23. Another additive to flour is calcium phosphate. This substance provides acid in the flour for persons who want to make sour milk or buttermilk biscuits. The added acid (between ¼% and ¾%) bolsters the leavening action of baking powder used for making these products.

Phosphated flour is used primarily for making _____.

sour milk or buttermilk biscuits

24. Mold inhibitors are added to bread (doughs) ingredients to discourage the growth of various molds and bacteria. Some bacteria form spores (bacteria with thick walls) that are not killed by baking. Under the right conditions of warmth and moisture these spores grow and turn pieces of bread into sticky, yellowish patches which can be pulled into rope, like threads. These rope spores can be held down by vinegar or other acids. Various molds also grow in bread products under the right conditions.

Propionates (salts of propionic acid) are added to baking formulas to combat the growth of molds and rope forming bacteria.

Mold inhibitors are additives used for the purpose of reducing the growth of _____ and _____.

spores and molds

25. Rope in bread is a condition caused by certain _____.

bacteria

38

inhibits

26. An acid condition <u>favors/inhibits</u> the growth of rope forming spores.

leavening agent

27. <u>Self rising</u> flour is used widely in the Southeast. It is flour that contains a leavening agent and salt.

Self rising flour is like any other flour except that the _____ has already been added.

Yes, this is done on occasion.

28. A special <u>gluten flour</u> or high gluten flour is made by adding extra protein to the flour so that it will have over 40% protein. Such flour can be added to ordinary flour to improve its baking quality or to produce high protein bread and rye breads.

Suppose you had a soft wheat flour, low in protein, which you wanted to use for making bread. Would it make sense to add some gluten flour to the weaker flour?

REVIEW

1. From which part of the wheat kernel does most of the flour come?

2. Which part of the wheat kernel is removed in most flour?

3. Why is whole wheat flour less stable than white flour?

4. The largest component of wheat flour is _____.

5. Protein content of flour varies from about _____ to _____.

6. Which of these flours will feel more gritty to the finger, the high protein or the low protein?

7. Rye flour has about the same protein as wheat flour, but little gluten can be developed in it. Why is this?

8. Soy flour is highly nutritious. Why don't we use more of it?

9. In what other products beside cakes is soft wheat flour likely to be called for?

10. "To soften" bread flour what would you add to it?

11. Which of these breads would use the "strongest" flour, French or American?

12. What is the advantage of bleached flour over unbleached?

13. When oxygen combines with the flour it matures it and also strengthens the gluten which will be developed. Potassium bromate added to the flour does the same thing. Does the baker add potassium bromate to his flour?

14. Potassium bromate is added to flour because it makes the gluten more _____.

15. Some flours lack sufficient enzymes to provide sugars on which the yeast can act. Name an additive that provides these enzymes.

16. Propionates are added to baking formulas for what purpose?

Water in Baking

gluten

1. Water is the liquid that makes possible the wetting of the protein in flour; this when mixed forms gluten. The water may come from the tap, or in milk or in eggs that are added.

Without water the development of _____ would not be possible.

gluten

2. Water is the agent which moistens the starch and sugar in bakery products, making it possible to form them into batters, pastes and dough.

Water acts as a mixing agent and is needed to moisten the proteins in flour so that _____ can be formed.

No, no gluten would form to provide the framework or structure of the cake or bread.

3. Could you bake a cake or bread without water?

slow down

4. The mineral content and acidity of the water used in baking may greatly affect the finished baked product. The acidity or alkalinity of the water in part determines the rate of fermentation of the dough or batter. Fermentation slows down when alkaline or hard waters are used. To overcome (neutralize) the alkalinity, more yeast can be added or an acid, such as vinegar, can be added. An alkaline water will speed up/slow down fermentation.

5. The degree of hardness is usually expressed as the number of parts per million of calcium carbonate present in the water.

DEGREE OF HARDNESS	PARTS PER MILLION CALCIUM CARBONATE
soft	10 - 50
slightly hard	50 - 100
hard	100 - 200
very hard	above 200

Hard water contains at least ____ parts per million of calcium carbonate.

6. Soft water contains less than ____ parts per million of calcium carbonate.

7. Water hardness can be measured in other ways too. The amount of calcium present is one such measure. The most common way of expressing the degree of water hardness is to talk in terms of the parts per million of _____

8. Water containing a small amount of minerals would be called _____water. That containing a large amount of minerals is _____.

9. Closely related to water hardness is the pH of the water, its degree of acidity. The acidity or alkalinity of liquid is measured in terms of an index number and expressed as pH. It is a short way of saying potential hydrogen and is a measure of the potential hydrogen concentration. The more hydrogen ions present, the more acid the product. Hard water is likely to be alkaline–but not always. Soft water can be slightly acid–but not always.

pH (degree of acidity) is related to the degree of water _____.

acidity -
alkalinity

10. The pH value of a liquid is expressed as a number between zero and fourteen. Pure water has a pH of 7. With a pH below seven, the water is said to be acid. The lower the pH, the more acid is the liquid.

When the pH is above seven the liquid is alkaline. The higher the pH, the higher the alkalinity.

pH is the measure of the _____ of water and other liquids.

High. The
lower the pH,
the more acid
the solution.

$$\frac{\text{pH}}{\text{11. } \quad 14 \qquad 7 \qquad 1}$$
alkaline   neutral   acid

The pH of any solution is a measure of its degree of acidity or alkalinity.

A low pH number indicates a high/low degree of acidity.

alkaline

12. Water with a pH of 8 would be on the acid/ alkaline side.

acid

13. Water with a pH of 6 would be on the acid/ alkaline side.

seven

14. Water that contains no minerals, or is completely "soft", has a pH of seven and is said to be neutral.

Since the amount of water added to bread dough represents a large proportion of the dough, even small quantities of minerals or other ingredients in the water can have marked effects upon the dough.

In general, water of medium hardness—from about 50 to 100 parts per million and slightly acid, is preferred for baking uses. Water for use in the bakery ideally would be of medium hardness and have a pH below_____ .

reduce (make the water less alkaline, more acid)

15. Excessively hard waters, those with high mineral content, may retard fermentation by toughening the gluten. The minerals present apparently prevent the proteins from absorbing water.

What can be done if the water you use is excessively hard?

1. Reduce the pH by adding vinegar or other harmless acid.

2. Use more yeast.

3. Decrease the dough improver (which contains minerals).

Vinegar added to an alkaline water will re-duce/increase the pH.

increase (to overcome the effect of hardness in the water)

16. When using very hard water it may be necessary to increase/decrease the amount of yeast used.

Probably not use any dough improver.

17. Dough improvers or conditioners will be discussed later. Let's just say that they include minerals and tend to increase the alkalinity of the dough.

If very hard water is used, we would probably not use/add more improver.

tighten or toughen it

18. Water that is too soft can result in sticky doughs. Minerals in hard water tighten the gluten. This condition seldom happens because of the use of dough improvers and yeast foods that add minerals to the water.

Minerals do what to gluten?

true

19. The hardness of water varies widely. In most parts of Florida, Utah, Arizona, New Mexico, South Dakota, Nebraska, and Iowa the water is quite hard. In Oregon, Washington and most of New England the water is quite soft. However, within a given area some of the water may be hard, some soft.

True or false: In hard water areas you may have to use water that has been treated to remove some of the minerals or you may have to add acid to the water to make it suitable for use in baking.

true

20. True or false: The hardness or softness in water used in bakeries can be important factors in the softness or pliability of doughs and can affect the rate of fermentation of yeast in the doughs.

the gluten

21. The pH (acidity) and hardness of the water used in baking affects the development of what important ingredient in dough?

Medium
7 (slightly acid)

22. In general we would like to have water for use in baking to be of _____ hardness and with a pH below _____.

False. It is likely to be too acid.

23. Water varies widely in its pH. Water stored in small reservoirs may accumulate leaves and grass that ferment and form carbon dioxide. This, in turn, creates an acid condition in the water. The pH of water in Amherst, Massachusetts, for example, may go as low as 5. In such cases it may be necessary to raise the pH by adding an alkali to the water.

True or false: Water with the pH of 5 is about right for baking purposes.

REVIEW

1. In order to develop gluten, we must have wheat flour and _____.

2. Alkaline water slows/speeds up the rate of fermentation.

3. The hardness of water is usually expressed as the parts per million of _____ contained in it.

4. Water that has a pH of 7 would be neutral/acid/alkaline?

5. Water that has a pH of 7.3 would be slightly alkaline/slightly acid.

6. If the water available for baking is excessively hard, it could be neutralized by adding vinegar. Another way of overcoming the effects of hardness is by using more/less yeast.

7. Dough improvers or conditioners increase/decrease the alkalinity of a dough.

8. Why is it that very soft water is not desirable for making a dough?

9. Suppose rain water (no minerals present) is used for baking. Would you expect the dough to be tough or sticky?

10. The two factors concerning water that is used for baking that are important are the amount of minerals present and the _____ of the water.

Bread and Other Yeast Products

flour, water
yeast and salt

1. In its simplest form, bread is wheat flour and water mixed together to form a dough and baked. Bread, as we think of it, is leavened with yeast and yeast grows and splits the sugars that are present to form carbon dioxide. This expands the dough as the dough bakes; the gluten and starches present in the dough become "firm" on baking and we have bread.

Bread, as we usually make it, contains salt, milk, shortening, sugar, and may have eggs added to it. The basic ingredients of bread are _____, _____, _____, and_____.

flour and water

2. Sweet doughs are similar to bread doughs except that flavorings and more sugar have been added. Some sweet dough formulas call for the addition of cake or pastry flour; this results in less gluten being developed and a less chewy product.

Rolls, coffee cake, and Danish pastry are similar to bread in that the basic ingredients are flour, yeast and water. Dozens of varieties of rolls and breads are possible to make, all similar in that the basic structure depends upon the flour and water dough.

To make bread products we start with ____ and_____.

hard wheat
flour, high in
protein and
gluten

3. Yeast doughs may be divided into rich and lean. Both contain flour, liquid, fat, salt and are leavened by yeast. A conditioner containing sugar may be added on which the yeast can feed.

The rich doughs contain greater amounts of sugar and fat, and sometimes eggs. Doughs to which any amount of sugar is added are called sweet doughs.

Lean dough products—bread, rolls, pizza—are characterized by a chewy texture and will therefore use what kind of flour?

gluten

4. Flour and water are mixed together to form a smooth mass, to develop the gluten and to distribute yeast cells uniformly throughout the dough so that they can receive proper nutrition.

Three purposes for mixing dough are (1) to form the dough into a workable mass, (2) to distribute the yeast cells and (3) to develop the ____.

the patent flour since this is the most finely ground of the flours and the most highly prized for baking.

5. The best wheat flours are called <u>patents</u> and the poorest <u>clears.</u> The patent flour (so named because it was obtained from a patented process) is the finest of the flours (has the smallest particles).

Soft or winter wheat produces a soft, velvety and powdery flour with more starch and less protein than the hard or spring wheat. A good flour from soft wheat has a clear white color. Soft flours are used for pastry, many quick breads, cakes and cookies. Hard wheat flour is slightly creamy in texture and has a gritty texture.

We use the hard wheat flours for bread, puff paste, and eclair paste. Soft wheat flour is used for cakes, cookies and muffins.

Which flour is likely to be the most expensive?

the one from hard wheat because it contains more protein

6. The amount of water absorbed by a dough is largely related to the amount of protein present.

Which dough would absorb more water, one made from hard wheat or one made from soft wheat?

There would be very little volume or structure in the bread, since rye flour develops no gluten.

7. Whole wheat bread is made from 40-60% whole wheat flour and 60-40% wheat flour.

To make regular rye bread, about 20% rye flour is used with 80% white flour, but some rye breads may contain as much as 50% or more of rye flour along with "high gluten" wheat flour.

What would happen if we used all rye flour?

The bread
crust becomes
tender, which
is not desirable
in such breads.

8. Hard, French, Italian and hearth breads are made with a crisp, chewy crust. To produce such bread, little or no shortening and sugar is used.

What will happen if shortening is added?

9. Bread is made by using the <u>straight dough method</u> or the <u>sponge method</u>. The straight dough method is one in which all the flour is added to the formula at one time and the dough is allowed to rise only once.

In the sponge method, about 40% of the flour is added after the dough has risen once. Sponge doughs are punched, given a second mixing and then given 15 to 25 minutes "<u>floor time</u>" during which some further fermentation takes place. Usually one minute is allowed for every one percent of the flour added in this second mixing.

Bread made by the straight dough method is allowed to rise only once; sponge doughs rise _____.

10. Straight doughs are fermented from 1½ to 2½ hours but sponge doughs are fermented longer.

Sponge dough is usually <u>made up</u> by large bake shops in horizontal high speed mixers. About 60% of the flour and all of the liquid and yeast are mixed together to form a thick batter. This is allowed to ferment at between 77-80° F. The dough doubles in bulk and becomes wavy or ripply so that at a slight touch it collapses. It is punched and the remaining flour, all of the salt, sugar, shortening, milk solids and conditioners are added and mixed.

The second fermentation period then takes place. This is usually referred to as "floor time", the dough dries out to the point where it can be handled. This is usually no more than 15-25 minutes. The dough rises but this is <u>not</u> regarded as a fermentation.

In the sponge dough process only about __% of the flour is mixed in the first stage.

11. In the <u>sponge dough method</u>, part of the flour, water, yeast, sugar and sometimes shortening are mixed, forming a dough called the sponge. The sponge is allowed to ferment for 3-4 hours, then is "remixed" with the remaining ingredients for final processing.

60% of the flour and all of the liquid and yeast.

In the <u>straight dough method</u> all of the ingredients are mixed at one time, allowed to rise and baked. In the sponge dough method, a <u>sponge</u> is made, made up of _____.

12. The principal advantage of the sponge dough method is that it allows greater flexibility. Sponges can be held longer without loss of quality in the bread. In contrast, straight doughs must be taken up and baked when ready (ripe). There is little leeway in either direction. If the dough has been fermented too much, it can be used only by adding it, a small portion at a time, to new doughs as they are mixed.

true

True or False: The sponge dough _method gives the baker a little more flexibility as regards when he must shape and bake the dough.

13. With a sponge dough, labor costs are <u>higher</u> because of "double handling". This is partly offset by the fact that about 20% less yeast is needed for a sponge dough than for a straight dough. The sponge dough can give greater volume in the bread and a more uniformly desirable texture in grain. For these reasons, large bakeries are likely to use the <u>sponge/straight</u> dough method of mixing.

sponge dough method

the sponge
dough method
since the fer-
mentation time
is longer.

14. After the dough is mixed, the critical factor in the rate of fermentation is the temperature of the dough. High temperatures speed up the action of the yeast; low temperatures retard the action.

In making a straight dough, the dough temperature should be between 78⁰ and 82⁰F.

In using the sponge dough method, dough temperature is lower, 72⁰ to 78⁰F, but after the remix, it should be 78⁰ to 80⁰F—no higher than 81⁰F.

Which method of mixing calls for a slower yeast action, the sponge or the straight dough method?

highly critical

15. The big reason why the temperature in doughs cannot be allowed to go above about 82⁰F is the fact that over-fermentation will take place and the doughs will become tacky or sticky. Once the dough has become sticky or tacky, it is almost impossible to mold and handle and will become "bucky".

Control of the dough temperatures thus becomes one of the most important functions of the baker.

Dough temperature after being mixed is highly critical/not so very important.

If it gets too
warm, there is
too much fer-
mentation.
The dough be-
comes very diffi-
cult to work.

16. Temperature of the dough continues to rise as it is being mixed; the heat results from the friction caused by mixing. To offset the increase in temperature, cold water or ice or both are added. Some mixing machines are surrounded by refrigerating coils or brine jackets to accomplish the same purpose.

Why worry so much about dough temperature?

17. To control the temperature of the dough, one must understand something about heat units. The heat unit used is the British thermal unit, Btu. A Btu is the amount of heat required to raise one pound of water one degree Fahrenheit.

If we have 25 pounds of tap water at 64° Fahrenheit and raise it one degree, how many Btu's have we introduced into the water?

18. If we have 100 pounds of dough at 79° Fahrenheit and wish to lower the temperature by 5 degrees, how many Btu's of energy must be removed from the dough?

19. In large bakeries dough temperature is controlled by refrigeration. The small bakery, however, controls the temperature by adding ice to the water in mixing. The ice and cool water is needed to offset the temperature rise created by the friction of mixing the dough. The longer the mixing time, the higher the temperature rise.

In adding ice, it should be remembered that when ice melts it absorbs 144 Btu's per pound of ice, even though the ice water formed is still at 32°F.

Suppose you add one pound of ice at 32°F to one pound of water at 64°F. Will the resultant temperature be half way between 32 and 64?

20. Yeast products are made in this sequence of operations: mixing, fermentation, punch, rest, make up, proof, and bake. Before mixing the ingredients are weighed, "scaled off" as the baker says, then formed into a smooth paste and the gluten is thoroughly developed.

What is the next step?

21. Yeast is used to make bread and sweet dough rise. Yeast action begins during the time the dough is allowed to ferment and ends in the oven when the internal temperature of the dough reaches around 140°F.

Ethyl alcohol is produced by the action of the yeast on some of the sugars in the dough. The yeast also releases carbon dioxide. The carbon dioxide is the main leavening agent in a yeast dough, although gases from water (steam) and ethyl alcohol may help some in the leavening.

Carbon dioxide gas is formed by the action of baking soda, baking powder and what other common baking ingredient?

22. As fermentation proceeds, the gluten hydrates (absorbs water) and the dough becomes more pliable and smooth.

Fermentation is considered complete when the dough has doubled in bulk.

The dough is "taken to the bench young", in other words, the dough is taken from the container where it is fermenting when fermentation is about ¾ complete.

Fermentation causes the dough to rise and become more _____ .

23. The next step is the punch. The dough has expanded to a point where the gluten cannot support the structure without the firming action of heat. If it is pushed or "punched", it collapses at that point.

In the "punch", the dough is folded over on all sides causing it to collapse and return to its original bulk. The punch allows the CO_2 formed to escape and redistributes the food available for the yeast so that a vigorous secondary leavening can take place.

Is the term "punch" misleading?

made up

24. The "make up" comes next. The dough is taken to the bench where it is allowed to "rest" a short time. It is then divided (cut), shaped and panned as desired. Rolled-in doughs have shortening spread over them and are folded and rolled at this point.

So far, the dough has been mixed, fermented, punched, had a rest, and _____.

make up

25. The next step is the "proof". Made up products are placed in an area where the temperature is about 100°F and the humidity is high. In a bake shop a "proofer" or proofing cabinet, in which steam or hot water produces a high humidity, may be used.

Leavening action increases, the yeast grows quickly giving off CO_2, and the products swell to at least twice the original make up size.

The "proof" follows what step?

yes; to avoid too much "oven spring" hearth and rye breads which develop hard, unyielding crusts are "docked", that is, sliced across the top to allow for expansion and to permit some of the gases to escape. If docking is not done, the crusts will burst.

26. Now, finally, the dough is ready to bake. As heat is applied, the final leavening occurs before the heat reaches 140°F and the yeast is destroyed. The steam and CO_2 produced rapidly expand the dough to produce "oven spring". The top crust of a loaf is pushed up because of the spring.

Would you guess that oven spring might be too vigorous if some of the gases were not allowed to escape?

no, their
smaller size
produces less
spring and ex-
cept for hard
rolls their
crusts are soft,
which permits
expansion.

27. Would you guess that small rolls should be docked?

fermentation,
punch, rest,
make up, proof
and bake

28. To review, we see that yeast dough products are made in a series of steps: mixing, _____, _____, _____, _____, _____ and _____.

flavor

29. The chart on the following page lists the basic ingredients of bread and the functions each performs in producing the final product.

We see that salt, in addition to being a flavoring agent, affects the fermentation process, the gluten and also the texture and grain of the bread.

Sugar also affects the fermentation and gives color to the crust.

Yeast, via the fermentation process, provides volume in the bread and also affects the texture and the grain. Yeast also provides some_____ .

BREAD INGREDIENTS AND THEIR FUNCTIONS

INGREDIENTS / **MAIN FUNCTIONS IN FINISHED PRODUCT**

INGREDIENTS	BINDING AGENT	ABSORBING AGENT	AIDS KEEPING QUALITIES	BACK BONE AND STRUCTURE	AFFECTS EATING QUALITIES	NUTRITIONAL VALUE	AFFECTS FLAVOR	AFFECTS FERMENTATION	AFFECTS GLUTEN	TEXTURE AND GRAIN	IMPARTS CRUST COLOR	AFFECTS SYMMETRY	VOLUME	PRODUCES TENDERNESS	ADDS QUALITY TO PRODUCT
BREAD FLOUR	X	X	X	X	X	X	X			X					
SALT							X	X	X						
SUGAR			X		X	X	X	X		X	X	X			X
SHORTENING			X		X	X					X	X		X	X
MILK SOLIDS			X			X	X			X				X	X
WATER	X														
YEAST							X			X			X		

Reprinted with permission of the publisher from J. Amendola's <u>The Baker's Manual for Quantity Baking and Pastry Making</u>, 2nd Edition. Copyright 1956 and 1960 by Ahrens Publishing Company, Inc.

insufficient
sugar

30. Many things can go wrong in the production of a loaf of bread. The left hand column in the facing chart lists these factors. The rest of the chart is concerned with pointing the finger at what could have caused a particular failure. For example, if the bread shows a gray crumb this could be caused by underproofing of the dough, the dough being too warm or the proof box being too hot.

A crust which is too thick may be caused by the dough being old, temperature of the oven being too low, the bread being overbaked or by _____.

improper
molding

31. If blisters appear in the crust of the bread, this can be caused by flour that has not been matured, dough that is too young or too old, or by _____.

the dough
being too old

32. If the crust of the bread has not developed a good brown color, this could have been caused by the temperature of the dough being too low, the proof box too hot, too little sugar being used or
_____.

a high temper-
ature—up to
600°F. to dry
the tomato
sauce and
quickly brown
the dough.

33. Baking temperatures are related to size of the product and to richness. Lean rolls and small products bake at 400°-425°F. Richer products and large, lean ones are baked at lower temperatures.

Pizzas which are a lean, thin product topped with tomato sauce and cheese require a high/low temperature.

no, they must
be baked daily
if a quality
product is
desired.

34. Depanning and cooling of yeast dough products should allow for the escape of steam and alcohol developed during baking. To allow for this, large products may be removed from their pans so that free air circulation can occur.

Hard crusted breads and rolls are not wrapped so as to prevent softening of the crusts. Does this mean that hard crusted bread and rolls will keep longer?

should not

35. Quality of bread can be properly maintained if bread is wrapped and frozen. However, refrigeration produces more staling than if the bread were kept at room temperature. In hot muggy climates refrigeration does prevent mold growth and may be necessary.

A pound and one half of unsliced bread that is frozen requires about 3 hours to thaw at room temperature.

Ordinarily we should/should not refrigerate bread.

BREAD, ROLLS

Many beginners in the baking trade are not enthusiastic about making bread and rolls because they feel the results are not as attractive as pastries and do not produce large profits. The commercial bakeries are doing a fine job in giving the public excellent quality breads.

There are, in addition to the standard breads, the specialty types of breads and rolls, some of which have the eye appeal and flavor to please the most fastidious gourmet. Examples of the latter may be found on the following pages.

Here are a few important rules to follow in making bread and rolls:

(1) Maintain absolute personal cleanliness.
(2) Use clean utensils, materials and machinery.
(3) Always use the very best quality ingredients.
(4) Keep a dough thermometer on hand for controlling the dough.
(5) Read all formulas carefully and scale all ingredients properly.
(6) Serve fresh products only, baked daily.

MIXING
The three purposes of dough mixing are as follows:

(1) To bring about a uniform mixture of ingredients and to form a smooth dough.
(2) To develop the gluten in the dough mass in order to promote the elasticity of the dough: the elasticity, in turn, will retain the gases formed by the yeast.
(3) To distribute the yeast cells uniformly so that they will receive proper nutrition.

The two principal methods of dough mixing are:

(1) Sponge dough method
Part of the flour, water, yeast, sugar and shortening are mixed, forming a dough called the "sponge" which is permitted to rise and ferment to the desired point. The sponge is then put back into the mixer and combined with the balance of the ingredients, i.e. the remainder of the flour, water, sugar, salt, milk, shortening and yeast. When this is mixed together into a smooth dough, it is again allowed to rise and is then divided into various sized pieces.

The sponge dough is suitable for larger commercial operations.

(2) Straight dough method
A straight dough is one in which all of the ingredients are put into the mixing bowl and mixed in a single operation. Dough is allowed to rise over a period of time that varies in accordance with the type of dough.

FERMENTATION

Fermentation takes place after the dough has been mixed and continues until the oven in which the bread or dough is mixed reaches a temperature of 138°F. At this point the yeast bacteria is dead and fermentation ceases.

The most favorable temperature for fermentation to take place is from 80° to 82°F. The period of fermentation depends on the amount of yeast used in the dough and the temperature of the room. The lower the temperature, the slower the fermentation; the higher the room temperature, the faster the fermentation takes place.

A dough that is not sufficiently fermented (under-proofed) is referred to as a young dough; dough that is over-proofed is known as an old dough.

Punching the dough is a process in which the gases developed during fermentation (carbon dioxide) are forced out of the dough. This helps to relax the gluten and equalizes the temperature of the dough.

The time to punch the dough is when it has doubled in size. Insert the open hand into the dough from 4 to 5 inches. If the dough recedes, it is ready for punching. If it springs back when the hand is inserted, longer fermentation is required. After the dough is punched, it must be proofed a second time before being made up into bread or rolls.

BREAD AND ROLL DOUGH PRODUCTION STAGES

Raw Materials
Weighing of Ingredients
Mixing
Fermentation Period
Scaling
Rounding
Bench Proofing
Moulding
Panning
Pan Proofing
Baking
Cooling

QUICK BREADS

The person who first named these popular members of the bread family remains a mystery. Why they are so named is obvious; they are easier to make and take less time than the ones made with yeast. What they are requires some special definition for there are so many of them. They are also called "hot breads" as well as by the name of the specific recipe used in producing them.

Quick breads can be classified by the type of leavening agent used. For example: biscuits, griddle cakes, scones, and shortcake are leavened by baking powder or baking soda. Popovers and Yorkshire pudding are leavened by steam.

Quick breads can also be grouped according to the thickness or thinness of the batter used to make them. There are "pour" batters, "drop" batters, and "soft" doughs which are to be rolled, patted out, or shaped. Popovers and waffles are made with pour batters. Corn bread, loaves, spoon breads and dumplings are made from drop batters, while some muffins and gingerbread are made from pour batters, others from drop. Scones, coffee cakes, tea breads, and doughnuts are made from soft doughs, and biscuits can be made from either drop batters or soft doughs.

Although these result in completely different breads, all are made of almost the same ingredients. They vary only because of the proportions used, and the way they are mixed and baked or cooked.

Further variety in quick breads comes from the diversity of cereal products used: wheat, whole wheat, rye, and corn flours, and bran, oatmeal or cornmeal. Any of these can be made into muffins, for example, yet each final baked product will taste and look different.

ORDINARY BREAD FAULTS AND THEIR CAUSES

CAUSES \ FAULTS	LACK OF VOLUME	TOO MUCH VOLUME	CRUST COLOR TOO PALE	CRUST COLOR TOO DARK	CRUST BLISTERS	SHELLING OF TOP CRUST	POOR KEEPING QUALITIES	POOR TEXTURE, CRUMBLY	CRUST TOO THICK	STREAKY CRUMB	GRAY CRUMB	LACK OF SHRED	COARSE GRAIN	POOR TASTE & FLAVOR
IMPROPER MIXING	X												X	
INSUFFICIENT SALT		X						X						X
TOO MUCH SALT	X													
DOUGH WT. TOO MUCH FOR PAN	X												X	
DOUGH WT. TOO LIGHT FOR PAN	X													
INSUFFICIENT YEAST	X							X			X	X		
TOO MUCH YEAST	X					X				X	X			
DOUGH PROOFED TOO MUCH							X	X		X	X		X	
DOUGH UNDER PROOFED		X					X	X	X			X		
DOUGH TEMP. TOO HIGH						X		X	X					
DOUGH TEMP. TOO LOW	X							X			X			
DOUGH TOO STIFF					X	X		X						
DOUGH TOO SLACK	X													
PROOF BOX TOO HOT					X									
GREEN FLOUR					X	X								X
DOUGH CHILLED		X				X	X	X						
TOO MUCH SUGAR				X			X	X			X	X		
INSUFFICIENT SUGAR	X	X	X	X	X		X	X			X	X	X	X
DOUGH TOO YOUNG			X	X				X				X		
DOUGH TOO OLD										X				
IMPROPER MOLDING	X				X									
INSUFFICIENT SHORTENING		X								X	X			
OVEN TEMP. TOO HIGH		X			X	X		X						
OVEN TEMP. TOO LOW			X						X	X				
OVER BAKED									X	X				

Reprinted with permission of the publisher from J. Amendola's The Baker's Manual for Quantity Baking and Pastry Making, 2nd Edition. Copyright 1956 and 1960 by Ahrens Publishing Company, Inc.

REVIEW

1. Flour and water are mixed to form a batter or dough. In the mixing what all-important protein substance is formed?

2. A sweet dough is like bread dough except that more _____ and flavorings are used in the sweet dough.

3. What ingredient in flour absorbs most of the water present?

4. True or False: A good volume rye bread contains wheat flour as well as rye flour.

5. How could you identify a hard wheat flour by feeling it?

6. Which of these flours—patent or clear—has the finest grain size?

7. Which flour—soft or hard—is used for each of these products:

> Cakes _____
> Bread _____
> Muffins _____
> Puff Paste _____
> Cookies _____

8. Most commercial bakers make bread using the <u>straight dough/sponge</u> method.

9. What are the advantages in using the sponge dough method?

10. Excessive dough temperature results in a _____ dough.

11. What unit of heat is necessary to raise one pound of water one degree Fahrenheit?

12. The more protein in the flour, the <u>more/less</u> water it can absorb.

13. Why do doughs rise in temperature when being mixed?

Basic Sweet Dough and Danish Dough

Basic sweet dough and Danish dough can be used to produce hundreds of varieties of baked goods. Variety can be obtained with these doughs by changing the fillings, i.e. using cheese, fruit, almond paste and also by varying spices, toppings, shapes, folding or twisting. No matter how they are varied, these are popular products.

Units of 1 to 2½ ounces are referred to as rolls or buns, among these are streusel buns, raisin cinnamon buns, Philadelphia sticky buns.

Larger units up to 12 oz. are referred to as coffee cake varieties: these include almond ring coffee cake, cinnamon ring coffee cake, meltaway coffee cake, etc.

Today it is more important than ever to define quality ingredients in terms of consumer acceptance. Therefore, select time-proven basic ingredients for your sweet dough from reliable manufacturers. There is no substitute for the best grades of flour, sugar, malt, syrup, salt, shortening, butter and milk, the highest quality frozen eggs, margarine, yeast and flavors.

PRODUCTION POINTS

BASIC SWEET DOUGH

Mixing—Now that we have selected top quality, consumer-accepted ingredients, the method of combining them to form a basic sweet dough is next in importance. To insure a uniform and thorough distribution of the sugar, shortening, salt, nonfat dry milk and flavor, it is suggested that they be creamed together thoroughly, however, not until light. Next, we add the egg product as fast as the creamed mass will absorb it. All of the water, with the exception of that used to dissolve the yeast, is then added and mixed in to break up the creamed mass. Add the flour and start mixing at slow speed. Immediately after adding the flour, the yeast solution is added and the mixing at slow speed continued until the bulk of the flour has been wet down.

The mixer may now be advanced to medium speed and the dough mixed until it is smooth and well developed. Should a firm dough be desired, it is suggested that approximately 25% of the flour be held back and added approximately 5 minutes before mixing is completed. This will prevent overheating. Firm doughs usually heat up rapidly and may become too warm before proper dough development has been attained.

Fermentation—Sweet yeast doughs should be given slightly less fermentation than is usually given bread and roll doughs. Slightly under-fermented doughs produce more desirable results than fully or slightly over-fermented doughs.

Sweet yeast doughs to be retarded should be given less fermentation than doughs that are to be made up in the usual manner. Sweet yeast doughs to be made up into individual units prior to retarding should be given ½ to ¾ fermentation. Dough to be cut up into strips and retarded should be given slightly less fermentation, as the larger units will require slightly more time for thorough chilling in the dough retarder than individually made up units.

Makeup—Complete details for makeup are given for the individual varieties. All varieties can be made up as small individual units or as coffee cakes, regardless of whether makeup directions specify one or the other.

Proofing—Sweet yeast dough products should be given full proof at a temperature ranging from 95º to 98ºF., and a relative humidity ranging from 80% to 85%.

Sweet yeast dough products that have been retarded as made up units should be allowed to warm up to room temperature before being placed in proof box. This will assure a rapid proof and good volume.

Baking—It is suggested that sweet yeast dough products be baked as quickly as possible, yet long enough to insure a thorough bake.

Finishing—It is recommended that, with few exceptions, all sweet yeast dough products be glazed as they come from the oven, glazing seals them, thus adding shelf life to the product. In addition to adding to the shelf life of the product, the glaze enhances the eating qualities and general appearance of products. Sweet yeast products should be cooled and packaged or placed in display cases as soon after baking as possible.

DANISH DOUGH

Naturally it is important that the ingredients used in making Danish Pastry be the best quality obtainable. Also, it is necessary that the formula used be in proper balance to meet the specific plant conditions.

Mixing—Danish pastry doughs should be mixed in the same manner as basic sweetdough, except that mixing should cease as soon as the materials have been thoroughly incorporated. Danish doughs are further developed during the rolling-in process.

Fermentation and Rolling-In Process—After mixing, scale off strips of an appropriate size and give them a 15 to 20 minute rest or fermentation period, preferably in the retarder.

Then sheet out the dough strips to a thickness of ½ to ¾ inch and in a sheet three times as long as wide. Spot butter or margarine shortening over 2/3 of the length of the dough sheet. Fold the unspotted third over the center third, and then fold the remaining third on top, making three layers of dough and two layers of shortening.

Again roll out to a thickness of approximately ½ inch and fold in thirds (no additional shortening is used). Allow pieces to rest 20 to 30 minutes in retarder.

Roll out and fold the dough in thirds twice more, with 20 to 30 minute rest period in the retarder between rollings. The dough must be kept cool during the rolling operation to prevent the margarine from soaking into the dough. Therefore, the amount of time in the retarder between rollings will depend on the room temperature.

After rolling and folding for the last time, it is advisable to allow the dough to rest 4 to 8 hours, preferably overnight, before starting makeup of the individual varieties. The best temperature for retarding is 35° to 45°F.

Makeup—All varieties of sweet dough products, with few exceptions, can be made up for greater richness from a rolled-in Danish dough. All varieties can be made up as small individual units or as coffee cakes regardless of makeup directions specifying one or the other.

Proofing—Danish pastry should be proofed at temperatures no higher than 90° to 95°F., and with only sufficient humidity to prevent the units from crusting.

Baking—As in the case of basic sweet yeast dough products, it is suggested that Danish dough products be baked as quickly as possible to insure a moist, good-eating finished product.

Finishing—It is also recommended that, with few exceptions, all sweet yeast dough products be glazed as they come from the oven, sealing them, thus adding shelf life to the product. In addition to adding to the shelf life of the product the glaze enhances its eating qualities and general appearance. Sweet yeast products should be cooled and packaged or placed in display cases as soon after baking as possible.

Danish pastry is similar to puff pastry except that yeast is used as a leavening agent. All purpose or a combination of bread and cake flour is used. Shortening is placed in a thin slab or dotted over the rolled-out dough. The dough is folded over the shortening and rolled several times. Between each rolling the dough is relaxed in a refrigerator for at least 20 minutes so that it can be better handled.

That brought
about by the
action of yeast.

The principal difference between Danish and puff pastry is in the leavening action. Danish makes use of what leavening action in addition to hot air and steam?

When Danish has been rolled and folded for the last time, allow it to rest for 4 to 8 hours or overnight before makeup. "Resting" is done in a retarder at 35° to 45°F. In resting the gluten strands relax and the dough can be more easily worked.

Indeed it is.

True or False: The production of Danish pastry is a time-consuming process.

REVIEW

1. What are some ways of adding variety to these products?

2. Once top quality consumer-accepted ingredients have been selected, what is the next important step in making a basic sweet dough?

3. Should sweet yeast doughs be given more or less fermentation than bread and roll doughs?

4. What should be the temperature and relative humidity range for proofing sweet yeast doughs?

5. How should sweet yeast dough products be baked?

6. Why is it recommended that all sweet yeast dough products be glazed as they come from the oven?

7. How does the mixing of Danish pastry doughs differ from that of basic sweet dough?

8. What is the principal difference between Danish and puff pastry?

9. How long should Danish be allowed to rest before makeup?

Puff Paste

Puff paste or "blatterteig," as it was originally called by the bakers of Germany where this delicacy originated, is made by alternately rolling and folding a fat into a previously made dough. The result after the series of rolling and folding stages is a sheet of dough with alternating layers of dough and fat.

The making of perfect puff pastry products is an art which can only be learned by close observation and practice.

REFRIGERATION AIDS PRODUCTION

For the making of puff pastry it is necessary that the materials be cold, therefore, the paste should be made up in a cool place. Modern mechanical refrigeration makes it possible to make up all the puff pastry products required for several days by placing the made-up pieces into the refrigerator and baking off such quantities as needed so that the product can be brought oven-fresh to the salesroom. This gives the retail baker the advantage of quality and freshness.

Puff pastry lends itself exceptionally well to refrigeration for two reasons . . . first, because of the solidifying nature of the fats, of which there is a great abundance; second, because of the fact that the dough has no leavening agent added, such as yeast or a gas-producing leavening agent, as is the case with sweet yeast raised dough or baking powder cakes.

LEAVENING

The leavening action of puff paste comes from three sources, as follows:

1. Vaporization of moisture in the dough and fat layers.

2. Enclosed air . . . When the dough is first rolled it contains very little air. However, each time it is folded over in the rolling process, a certain percentage of air becomes enclosed with it. These air cells expand during baking, thus assisting in the leavening of the product.

3. Bubbling of fats . . . When subjected to baking temperature the fats form air bubbles and boil. These bubbles assist in raising the dough.

Acids such as cream of tartar, lemon juice or vinegar are not, in a sense, added as leaveners, yet they do contribute to the leavened condition of the finished products because of the effect they have in causing the protein or gluten of the flour to become more elastic, thus enabling it to stretch rather than break.

The addition of one egg for each pound of flour also increases the leavening power, this power coming principally from the egg whites. The yolks add richness and color to the product.

Many bakers prefer not to use acid in a puff paste dough when it is to be held in the refrigerator either in dough form or in shaped units and baked off over a period of time as needed. The reason for this is that products made from retarded puff paste dough have less volume when an acid is added than is the case when the acid is omitted.

FLOUR–FATS

The flour should be a good bread flour, or a blend may be used of two-thirds bread flour and one-third cake flour in the event the bread flour should prove too strong.

The fat should be of a tough nature. There are many good margarines on the market made specifically for puff paste and these margarines give the finished product an appearance which excels that of a product in which butter alone is used. In combining a portion of each, the baker is able to have both flavor and appearance.

Rolling Process: To begin rolling-in of the fats, dust the table and the dough with flour, roll out into an oblong sheet three times as long as it is wide, to a thickness of one-half inch. Care must be taken that corners are square. Brush off excess flour.

Place the fats in small pats or discs over two-thirds of the area. Now fold the bare or uncoated part over half of the coated part, then fold this over the remaining coated dough so that there are two layers of fat and three layers of dough. Press down the ends and sides with rolling pin to seal in the fats. This now forms an oblong or square. Lift this sheet or block around lengthwise carefully.

Dust again with flour and begin rolling out carefully with not too great a pressure on the pin (at no time should rolling pin be borne down upon) to a sheet of not less than one-half inch thick and the same length as the sheet was before the folding process. Corners must be rolled square. Brush off excess flour and fold sheet in three. Place on cloth-covered pan or board, cover with moist cloth or greased paper, and permit to rest for at least 15 minutes in refrigerator or other cool place.

Care must be taken that the dough does not remain refrigerated too long in the early stage of rolling and folding, since this would cause the fat to solidify as it is still somewhat in pats, having received only one roll. Should this happen, then at the next rolling stage these solidified fat particles would crust through the layers of dough. This is very undesirable. After the second roll the fats have commenced to be sheeted and the danger of breaking through is lessened.

After the dough has rested for the required length of time the rolling and folding process is repeated until a total of five rollings and foldings, including the original one, have been made.

It is essential to allow the fifteen-minute rest period between each rolling and folding stage because, immediately after rolling, the dough is quite tough and elastic and if you were to roll and fold right in succession, the dough would be so tough and elastic that great pressure would have to be put onto the rolling pin. This would not only be extra hard to do but the layers of fats and dough would have a tendency to crush into each other, causing breaks. In resting, the dough becomes soft and pliable, enabling the baker to continue rolling and folding with ease and lessening the danger of crushing the layers into one another.

Practice and observation will determine if one more turn or fold-in-two is required. As a rule, if the fats run out during baking, then one more half-fold may be given. If, on the other hand, the goods made from the paste bakes out too tight or heavy, then the dough has been worked too much and should have received one rolling and folding less. If not quite certain that the dough has received sufficient rolling and folding, a small piece may be baked off in a pie plate to test it.

Due to the fact that the original shape of puff paste from the first rolling and folding stage is oblong, there is a tendency to roll the dough throughout the entire process of rolling and folding in one direction, namely, lengthwise. This causes the formation of strands that naturally will flow in the direction in which the rolling was done. This condition is objectionable and to prevent it the rolling-in should be done in two directions—lengthwise and breadthwise—or roll in the direction of the length of the bench and alternate by rolling at a right angle to the bench length, in a crisscross manner.

After the final rolling stage, the dough should rest at least one hour before making up into shapes, and the shaped units should be allowed to rest at least 30 minutes before baking.

1. Puff pastry consists of many layers, usually over 1,000. It is high in fat and leavened completely by steam and hot air. It is made by incorporating a large amount of fat into a dough and by repeated foldings and rollings (usually at least 3 or 4 rollings) the many layers are formed. It is used for making patty shells and their big brothers the vol-au-vent, creme horns, creme slices, turnovers, Napoleons, and for top crusts when a high rise, short crust is wanted. The baked puff pastry is delightfully crisp, many layered, and tasty.

None is added. Steam and hot air expand the many layers of dough.

What leavening agent is used in puff pastry?

2. In the continental kitchen, puff paste is known as "feuilletes" which means "many leaves". This is an apt description because the identifying characteristic of puff pastry is the fact that it is made of a thousand or more layers of thinly rolled dough and is, therefore, tender.

We need high gluten development, therefore, bread flour. Some of the older recipes still call for a weaker flour. If weaker flour is used, the product has fewer layers but is more tender.

To get the thin layers required, what kind of flour would you think would be used?

3. Modern puff pastry formulas call for bread flour, fat, eggs, water and salt. The eggs also help in forming the layers.

Because the dough puffs or rises rapidly when exposed to high temperature.

Many recipes call for a .75% cream of tartar which helps to tenderize the gluten and make a whiter dough.

Often the fat used in modern formulas is a special puff pastry shortening. It comes in sheets ready to be laid over the rolled dough.

Why the name puff pastry?

hot air and
steam

4. No other baked product is quite like puff paste. It contains no sugar or leavening agent, yet it can rise to 8 times its original size. A quarter inch of puff pastry dough may rise to over 2 inches in thickness.

Puff pastry is thin strands of gluten and eggs separated by fat and leavened by _____.

it will be too
hard and punc-
ture the dough.

5. Getting the shortening into the dough can be done in two ways, but is usually accomplished by "rolling in", spreading the fat evenly on the rolled surface of the dough.

The dough and the shortening should be at about the same consistency so that the shortening will not break into and rupture the walls of the dough when rolled.

Care must be taken that every bit of fat is evenly distributed through the dough.

If the room is warm, the dough must be kept refrigerated after it has been rolled and the fat must not be less than 60°F. or it will puncture the dough walls.

In making up puff pastry, temperature of the dough must not be too high or the dough will puncture; temperature of the fat must not be too high because it will become oily and will not spread.

Temperature of the fat must not be too low because _____.

Yes, this is
true. This is
one reason
why puff pas-
try is often
purchased
already made,
ready to be
formed and
baked.

6. After fat is rolled into the dough, the dough and fat are allowed to rest for at least 20-25 minutes under refrigeration to allow the gluten strands to adjust to the new length and to keep the dough and fat at the same temperature. The dough is rolled and rested several times.

Is making up puff pastry a time-consuming and costly process?

REVIEW

1. Puff pastry is made from a stiff dough which is <u>high/low</u> in fat.

2. Why add cream of tartar to a puff pastry formula?

3. What leavening agent is contained in a puff paste formula?

4. Why is it important to keep puff pastry comparatively cool?

5. What will happen to the fat used in puff pastry if it is too warm?

6. Some puff pastry formulas call for the inclusion of eggs. Why?

7. Danish pastry and puff pastry are alike in that layers of dough are formed. They are different in that <u>Danish/puff pastry</u> is yeast leavened.

Pie Making

Any dish of fish, flesh, fowl, or fruit covered on top with a crust of some sort is a pie. In America, pies are more often than not dessert pies, baked in a shallow pan with a bottom crust. In England, this type of pie is known as a tart. There are many kinds of crusts used for pies: crumbs, meringues, biscuits, as well as regular pastry. There are even pies such as Shepherd's Pie where the "crust" consists of mashed potatoes. Many pies are, in fact, not covered with a crust at all, but rather baked in a pastry shell leaving the top exposed. There seem to be as many varieties of pie as there are women of many nations who bake pies.

Americans inherit their love of pies from the English. In the 14th century, London was full of cookshops selling deep-dish meat pies with a heavy crust. The famous English mince pie, the Christmas pie that Little Jack Horner ate in his corner, evolved from these early meat pies. An old English tradition claims that eating twelve mince pies, one each day from Christmas until Twelfth Night, will make the eater happy for twelve months of the year.

When the colonists came to this country they brought with them their love for the English meat pies and dessert tarts. Until the Revolution, women continued the custom of baking pies in deep pastry shells covered with a top or "coffin". Sometime after we declared our Independence, a thrifty New England housewife realized that flat pies, or "tarts", needed less filling, and now the traditional American pie is a flat one.

Several pies are particularly associated with the United States. There is the pumpkin pie, a refinement of the first pumpkin pies that were merely hollowed-out whole pumpkins; the molasses-flavored shoo-fly pies of the Pennsylvania Dutch; and most famous of all—American apple pie. In the days before refrigeration and freezers, the apples were picked, peeled, quartered, and hung on cords in the kitchen. The dried quarters of apple were used to make pies all through the winter. New Englanders ate them for breakfast.

"What is pie for?" asked Emerson when challenged on the custom. In 1902 the New York Times blasted an English suggestion that pie be eaten only twice a week. This, said the Times, was "utterly insufficient. . .as anyone who knows the secret of our strength as a nation and the foundation of our industrial supremacy must admit. Pie is the American synonym of prosperity, and its varying contents the calendar of the changing seasons. Pie is the food of the heroic. No pie-eating people can ever be permanently vanquished."

PIE CRUSTS

There are two basic types of pie crust:

(1) Flaky pie crust
(2) Mealy pie crust

Although the flaky crust may contain identical ingredients of the same proportions, the results may be quite different.

When a flaky crust is desired, rub the flour and shortening together until they become nuggets the size of walnuts before adding the liquid and salt.

When a mealy crust is desired rub the flour and shortening until there is a finer distribution of the shortening throughout the flour.

INGREDIENTS FOR PIE CRUST

Always use a soft wheat flour, such as pastry flour, for pie crust. If a stronger flour is used, it must be worked with a higher proportion of fat. That is why pastry flour is recommended.

Shortening or fats used in making pie crust must be of plastic consistency. Lard is a good choice, but there are many people who object to the taste. Thus the most popular fat is vegetable shortening. A proportion of butter greatly improves the flavor and should be used where the cost factor does not become too serious. Water must always be very cold when used for making pie crust. The salt is usually dissolved in the water.

Thus the essential ingredients that go into the making of good pie crust are as follows:

Pastry flour
Vegetable shortening, some butter when possible.
Salt
Cold water

In some formulas other ingredients such as vinegar and baking powder are suggested. These ingredients do not improve the pie crust.

NOTE: Pie dough should not be overmixed.

PIE TRIMMINGS

When pie crusts are being rolled out, care should be taken to keep the size of each piece as close as possible to the size of the pans, thus keeping pie trimmings to a minimum. Pie trimmings should not be used to make up more than 50% of the piece of dough and should be used for bottom crusts only.

PIE WASHES

Milk, cream, eggs and milk, melted butter and water are the various kinds of pie washes used to improve eye appeal of pie crusts. The type used depends upon the finish required on the particular product.

THICKENING AGENTS

Starches and flours are used as thickening agents in pie fillings. Starches are used more often because they do not have a tendency to discolor and become gummy.

The amount of starch used varies and depends upon the jelling quality of the starch, the amount of liquid in the filling and the desired consistency of the finished pie.

From two to five ounces of cornstarch per quart of liquid (juice plus water) is the approximate amount used in preparation of the different fillings.

Care should be taken to cook the starch until the mixture is transparent and shiny: mixture should be removed from heat when it starts to boil.

PIE FILLINGS

There are five main types of pie fillings:

(1) Fruit pie
(2) Cream pie
(3) Chiffon pie
(4) Soft pie
(5) Specialty pies

FRUIT PIES

The most popular fruit pies are Apple, Pineapple, Apricot, Peach, Prune, etc. The fruit used may be fresh, frozen, canned, dried or prepared pie filling.

FILLING PREPARATION

Among the many methods used in filling pies today, the following three are the most generally accepted:

(1) Cooked Juice Method

    (a) Drain juice from fruit and bring to a boil.

    (b) Thicken with proper amount of dissolved cornstarch.

    (c) Bring back to a boil to clarify or assure proper setting of the starch.

    (d) Add granulated sugar, salt, spices, butter or other flavoring agents and stir until dissolved.

    (e) Pour over drained fruit, stir carefully and do not crush the fruit.

    (f) When the filling is cold it is ready for the pies.

The above method is generally used for Cherry, Apple, Blueberry, Apricot and Peach pies.

(2) Cooked Fruit and Juice Method

    (a) Bring juice and fruit to a boil.

    (b) Add the amount of dissolved cornstarch needed to bring juice and fruit to a proper consistency. After the cornstarch is added, always bring the filling back to a boil so that it will clarify.

    (c) Add the desired amount of sugar and stir until thoroughly dissolved. Care should be taken when cooking the fruit to stir occasionally to prevent the possibility of scorching.

    (d) When the filling is cold it is ready for the pies.

The above method is generally used for Raisin, Pineapple and also Apple if the latter are unusually hard.

(3) Home Made Method

    (a) Mix the fruit with spices, flour and sugar.

    (b) Fill the unbaked pie shells.

    (c) Place a lump of butter or margarine on top of the filling.

    (d) Cover the pie and bake as usual.

This method is very simple. However, the flour in the filling has a tendency to remain uncooked. Therefore, the consistency is not as easily controlled as in the preceding two methods.

CREAM PIE FILLING

Vanilla, Chocolate, Butterscotch, Banana and Coconut are the most popular cream pies. Care should be taken to acquire a good smooth cream with a delicate flavor. This cream filling is always placed into pre-baked pie shells.

CREAM PIE METHOD

(a)   Place milk with part of the sugar in a round bottomed pan and scald.

(b)   Take egg yolks, balance of sugar, starch and flavor and mix into a paste. Add to this part of the milk to make the mix into liquid form.

(c)   When part (a) is near the boiling point, add part (b) and continue to stir until it reaches a boil, then remove from the heat.

(d)   Add necessary flavor to batter and stir.

(e)   Place in pre-baked pie shells.

(f)   After cooling, top with meringue or whipped cream.

CHIFFON PIE FILLING

Chiffon pies are mixed in a manner similar to fruit pie method (2) or cream pie filling. Meringue is folded into this mixture.

Both cream pies and fruit pies may be converted into chiffon pies.

CHIFFON PIE METHOD

(a)   Place in a pan the fruit, sugar, flavor, color, salt, water or milk and bring to a boil on top of the stove.

(b)   Dissolve the starch in juice or water, mix with part (a) and continue to boil.

(c)   Remove from heat.

(d)   Make meringue with egg whites and sugar.

(e)   While above mixture is still hot <u>immediately</u> fold in the meringue.

(f)   Place mixture into pre-baked pie shell. Remember to fill the shell generously.

Pyramid the filling into the shell with a spatula.

(g)   Allow to cool and top with whipped cream.

SOFT PIE FILLING

Pumpkin, sweet potato, squash, custard and pecan pies are soft pies. They require a deep pie plate with an additional fluted pie crust rim.

Soft pies are made with an unbaked crust.

An uncooked filling is made which is set during the baking process. The filling contains eggs which help to coagulate the filling during baking.

SPECIALTY PIE FILLING

Nesselrode, ice cream and Boston cream pies are Specialty pies. They are a combination of the foregoing methods.

1. The broad definition of a pie is any dish of meat or fruit covered with or baked in a dough crust. In the bakery we are concerned with dessert pies, baked in a shallow pan with a bottom crust, and often with a top crust. Crusts are made from crumbs, meringues, biscuits, but the one with which we are concerned is a short pastry dough.

When we say "short", we mean what?

The dough contains a relatively high proportion of fat.

2. A common way of classifying pies is according to the filling used. Fillings can be divided into fruit, cream, chiffon, soft fillings, such as pumpkin or custard, and fillings for specialty pies such as for ice cream pie. A chiffon pie is similar to a fruit or a cream except that beaten egg whites and sugar have been folded into the filling to "leaven" it.

How would you classify a strawberry chiffon pie?

As a chiffon pie since it is a foamy filling created by folding in the beaten egg whites.

3. Pies can also be divided into those that have the shell and the filling baked together and those for which the shell and filling are prepared separately. Chiffon, cream, lemon meringue and most specialty pies use pre-baked shells. These shells are best made from a mealy crust.

Soft pies such as pumpkin, custard, and pecan are baked crust and filling together. The bottom crust should be "mealy". The richer in shortening, the less likely that bottom soakage will occur.

Most fruit pies are baked crust and filling together.

True or False: Pie crusts are usually baked separately for chiffon, cream and specialty pies.

True

4. Why not bake the filling and the crust together when making a chiffon pie?

The chiffon filling containing beaten egg whites would be over-cooked while the shell was still baking.

The fat.

5. Pie dough is usually made from pastry flour (medium protein content), a plastic shortening, salt and cold water.

Fat constitutes from 25% to 40% of the pie crust formula.

When baked, pie dough is a relatively compact (unleavened) dough (unlike cake or bread) which breaks easily when eaten.

What ingredient in pie dough makes for a tender crust?

mixing

6. Pie crusts are of two basic types: flaky and mealy.

They both may contain exactly the same ingredients, but the method of mixing is different.

Flaky crust is made by mixing the flour and half the shortening into a complete blend, then adding the rest of the shortening and mixing into pea-sized or larger balls of fat surrounded by the flour-shortening blend. Water is added and the mixing completed. When the dough is baked, the fat melts and the steam generated separates the layers. The resulting crust is layers of dough, separated by the fat.

Mealy crust is well mixed. The shortening is distributed throughout the flour (Mix ½ flour with all shortening, then the rest of flour—then the water.)

Differences between a mealy and a flaky crust are normally the result of the method of_____.

The crust
would be tough
because too
much protein
is present. You
would have to
add more shor-
tening to tender-
ize the gluten
strands.

7. Lard at one time was the popular shortening for use in pastry. Today, vegetable shortening, despite its higher cost, is used more frequently. Some butter and/or margarine may be added for flavor and/or color.

From what you know, what would happen to a pie dough if we use bread flour?

tough

8. In mixing pie dough develop the gluten only to the point where it will hold the dough together when rolled. If over-mixed, too much gluten is developed. There is excessive shrinkage when the crust bakes. The crust is likely to be_____.

There would be
no gluten dev-
elopment and
the dough
would not roll
out. You
would have a
roux (fat and
flour mixture).

9. Very cold water—usually ice water—is used when mixing pie dough so that the gluten development is depressed during mixing. The cold water allows enough mixing to distribute the water evenly without making for a tough dough. Salt and any dextrose used is dissolved in water so that it will be evenly distributed in the dough.

What would happen if no water were used?

No, because
there is not suf-
ficient gluten
development to
hold the dough
together for
proper rolling.

10. Can we successfully use cake flour for making pastry?

False.

11. Some bakers feel that to make a flaky crust it is necessary to hand mix the flour and the fat. This takes too long, is costly in labor, and not particularly sanitary. A special dough mixing machine "Artifax" was developed in Sweden and is available in this country. The mixing arms scoop up the dough in a manner similar to what would be done in mixing the dough by hand. Small commercial batches can be successfully mixed on low speed in a regular up-right mixer with a paddle.

The key to making a flaky crust is to avoid over-mixing the flour and fat and stopping when the balls of fat and flour are of the size desired.

True or False: A flaky crust can be made only by hand mixing the fat and the flour.

It gets tough because too much gluten is developed.

12. Fat used in making pie dough should be at about 70°F. If the fat is appreciably colder, it is apt to be too hard and will break and tear the gluten strands. If too hot, it becomes oily and over-blends with the flour.

Once water is added, mix as little as possible.

What happens if pastry dough is over-mixed?

Yes, more butter than vegetable shortening is needed to do the same shortening job.

13. Excessive water in a pastry dough causes toughness, possibly because the gluten takes on too much water and because it requires more mixing to develop the dough to the point where it will be "workable". Most water in a pie dough is absorbed by the gluten, not the starch. Butter contains up to 20% water. If butter is used, should some allowance be made for the water in the butter?

False; just enough to form a dough which will roll.

14. The use of ice water for pie dough prevents the gluten from developing as fast as it would in a warm dough.

True or False: We want plenty of water in a pie dough.

The dough is more densely packed and will not become soggy as quickly as a flaky pastry.

15. Leftover dough can be used for making a mealy dough (commonly used for bottom crust). The mealy dough is preferable for use in making cream and custard pies. Why?

Mealy and tough.

16. A flaky dough becomes what kind of dough when mixing is continued?

To allow it to adjust to the new extended length of the gluten strands.

17. In rolling out dough, the dough is sometimes rolled thin, then allowed to relax or rest. The gluten strands have been stretched excessively. During the relaxing period, the gluten strands shorten somewhat, but not back to their original length. The dough can then be rolled again and stretched farther. Strudel dough, which is stretched to paper thinness, must be relaxed between rollings and uses bread flour for maximum gluten development.

A dough is relaxed for what reason?

PREVENTING A SOGGY BOTTOM CRUST

So that the crust will not be soaked.

18. If a flaky crust is wanted for a pre-baked shell, fill the shell only a short time before serving the pie.

Why?

Yes, the bottom is hotter and the crust will bake more quickly sealing out the juices.

19. To minimize soakage in the bottom crust of a fruit pie, would it be a good idea to bake the pie on the bottom shelf of the oven?

20. Use of a shiny pie tin may result in a soggy bottom crust. Why?

A shiny surface reflects heat and retards baking time. Some frozen pie bakers used to "ink" the outer bottom of the "tin". Some still employ a dark metal for the bottom.

21. To prevent the bottom crust from soaking, dry cake crumbs can be put in the bottom of the pie before filling it. The crumbs absorb excess liquid from the fruit, liquid that would otherwise soak into the crust. High shortening content is a good deterrent to bottom soaking.

put some dry cake crumbs in the bottom of the pie before filling it. Or use more shortening for the bottom crust.

To avoid soggy bottom crust in a pie, bake the pie in the bottom of the oven, use a mealy crust, or

_____ .

OVEN TEMPERATURES

22. Temperatures vary within the oven, they are hotter near the bottom; cooler at the top. Some electric ovens have both top and bottom heat sources and the temperatures vary according to the heat produced at the top and bottom.

Heat is applied at the bottom of the oven creating a higher temperature near the bottom.

In a gas oven why does the temperature vary within the oven?

23. Oven temperatures are not always what is read on the temperature control knob (the thermostat). Check the thermostat by placing a mercury thermometer in the oven. The thermostat and the thermometer should read the same. If not, calibrate (change) the thermostat to read the same as the thermometer.

Do not use a spring thermometer, it will lose its accuracy with the slightest jar.

What is used to check the accuracy of the thermostat (the knob control)?

24. Suppose an oven is too hot at the bottom. A sheet pan placed on the lowest oven rack will even out the temperature. Most places put pies in sheet pans to bake, a practice known as panning. If the bottom heat is still too high, they may "double pan". Also, it makes a big difference if the sheet pan is new and shiny, or blackened by "ink". If heat is applied from both bottom and top, reduce the bottom heat.

Would you expect a convection oven (one with a rotor fan in the back) to be more even in temperature throughout the oven?

25. The kind of filling used in a pie determines the oven temperature to use. Fruit pies are usually baked at 400-425°F. for 25-30 minutes.

Some bakers prefer 350-375°F. for 45 minutes.

Custard pies and others using a quantity of milk and eggs must have special handling. Custard pies baked directly in the shell are baked for 10 minutes at 450°F. Then the temperature is reduced to 300°F. and the baking continued for 45-50 minutes to cook the custard.

What will happen to an egg and milk filling if the high heat is continued?

26. Why not use micro-wave ovens for baking pies?

These ovens produce energy so fast that the inside of the pie is overcooked before the crusts become barely warm.

27. Remember, the fruit in baked pies is already cooked. The problem is to bake the crust to a golden brown and reheat the filling. This usually takes 45-55 minutes using a 425°F. oven.

At 425°F. the filling is likely to be over-cooked, the crust too dry and per-haps burned.

What would happen if you bake such pies longer than an hour?

STARCH THICKENERS

28. Starches are widely used in the bakery for thickening pie fillings, and also for thickening custards and puddings in the bakeshops of restaurants.

No, since the fruit would not usually be seen and the gel is too rigid.

The most widely used starch in this country is that of corn. There are two types, regular cornstarch and that made from waxy maize, a special type of corn.

Regular cornstarch has a high thickening power, but its gel is relatively cloudy or opaque.

Would you want to use regular cornstarch for fruit pies?

29. Would regular cornstarch be suitable for cream or lemon pies?

Yes, this is the most commonly used starch.

30. On the next page granules of waxy maize starch are magnified 500 times.

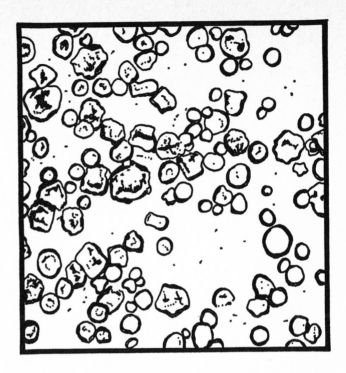

Waxy maize and other cornstarches are modified by cross-linking the molecules of starch. As a result of this cross-linking, the granules are more resistant to breakdown in the cooking and handling processes.

cloudy; clear   The modified waxy maize starches produce pastes which are water-clear, viscous and cohesive. After cooking and cooling they form weak gels.

Modified waxy maize starches are excellent for use in thickening fruit pie fillings.

Regular cornstarch which has been cooked and cooled forms a_____gel, while modified waxy maize starch forms a_____ gel.

31. Some bakeshops are using pre-cooked starches, also known as instant or pre-gelatinized starches. They have already been cooked and have been dried. When water is added, the water is immediately absorbed by the starch granules.

Fruit pies, especially those like strawberry pie in which it is desirable to retain the appearance and form of the fruit.

Although pre-cooked starches cost more, they save the time usually taken in cooking, cooling and handling of the usual starch.

The natural flavor of the fruit is protected in the preparation of fruit pie fillings and the fruit tends to retain its natural shape and appearance because it is cooked only once.

Pre-cooked starches would likely be used in thickening what kind of pies?

32. In using pre-cooked starches, the starch must be blended with sugar and other dry ingredients before adding liquid. Otherwise the starch will lump when water is added.

True

"Instant pies" can be made by using pre-cooked starch and pouring a filling into baked pie shells.

True or False: Instant starch has already been cooked and has been dehydrated.

33. Pre-cooked starch can be used to stabilize whipped cream. The whipped cream will not separate for several days if it is refrigerated.

Yes, the pre-cooked starch soaks up water very fast and will lump if not separated by the sugar.

Would you guess that the pre-cooked starch would have to be blended with sugar before being added to whipped cream?

34. Pre-cooked starch can also be substituted for part of the flour in cakes to improve eating quality or to help retain moisture.

The starch granules soak up and retain moisture.

Why is pre-cooked starch a good stabilizer for whipped cream?

gelatinization

35. When heat is applied to starch and water the granules begin to swell and take up the water. This process is called <u>gelatinization</u>. The larger granules swell first at lower temperatures; the smaller granules gelatinize at a higher temperature. Regular cornstarch begins to gelatinize at about 147°F., but complete gelatinization does not take place until the solution reaches about 200°F.

The technical name for the thickening of a starch and water solution is_____.

waxy maize

36. Regular cornstarch completes its thickening at about 200°F. As it cools, it thickens further and forms a gel which is more rigid than the paste formed during the initial thickening. This is a disadvantage in that the baker cannot tell for sure how rigid the gel will be until it has cooled and set.

Waxy maize starch has no second thickening and its consistency, therefore, can be better controlled by the baker.

Which starch is more easily controlled as regards final consistency, waxy maize or regular cornstarch?

overcooking;
over stirring

37. Over-cooking of a starch causes the granules to rupture which thins out the solution. Many a pie filling has been ruined because of overcooking of the starch. Excessive stirring of a starch solution during cooking also ruptures the starch granules and causes the paste to thin out.

Two practices to avoid in cooking starch are: (1)_____and (2)_____.

Cook the
starch sepa-
rately so that
the acid will
not interfere
with the gelat-
inization.

38. Acid ingredients in the pie filling destroy the thickening power of the starch and prevent it from "setting".

To avoid this, add the acid ingredients after the starch has thickened. Then cool the solution as quickly as possible because slow cooling of paste solution with a high pH also makes for a runny solution.

In making a filling for a gooseberry pie (low pH), would you cook the starch separately and then add it or cook the starch with the gooseberries?

more

39. Too much sugar also interferes with gelatinization.

To avoid such interference add the sugar to be used in two stages. Add only part of the sugar to the starch-water solution and cook it. After the gelatinization has taken place the other sugar can be added.

Other ingredients such as fat, salt, eggs and dry milk solids weaken a starch gel.

When large amounts of sugar, fat or dry milk solids are called for, the recipe needs <u>more/less</u> starch to achieve a particular thickening level.

under cooking
of the starch
and water solu-
tion.

40. Pie fillings and puddings thickened by starch sometimes "weep" after setting a while. Water that has only been partially absorbed by the starch separates from the starch and the gel may collapse or lose its consistency. This is usually caused by failure to completely cook the starch solution so that the water is firmly bound into the starch granules.

Weeping is likely to be caused by_____.

41. Puddings and pie fillings thickened with starch that are to be frozen should be made using the waxy maize starches or other starches which have been specially modified and will withstand freezing without separating.

Very true, because many of the new items available such as invert sugar and the modified starches will produce superior baked products.

Numerous starches have been tailored for the bakeshop and the baker is well advised to purchase those that are recommended for particular pie fillings and puddings even though they cost somewhat more than regular cornstarch.

True or False: As bakery ingredients are improved and new ones are developed for specific uses in baking, the baker should at least try them out rather than only using "tried and true recipes and ingredients".

AVOIDING BLISTERS IN THE SHELL

42. Blisters tend to form in a crust that is baked in a pie pan. To avoid these, holes are made in the dough before baking, a process called <u>docking</u>.

dock (blisters will also form because of excessive moisture in the dough)

Another way of avoiding blisters is to double pan the dough. An empty pie tin is placed on top of the dough in the pan. Double panning holds the crust in place.

To avoid blisters forming in a pie shell, double pan or _____the dough before it is baked.

43. Double panning is the recommended way to make pie shells, the single bottom crusts. By placing a pan inside the shell while the crust bakes, the crust is held in place and the proper shape is held.

shape or form

Double panning helps to avoid blisters in the shell and also holds the_____of the shell while it bakes.

On the bottom rack where the temperature is highest.

44. Frozen pies are raw crusts containing a cooked filling that is frozen solid. The problem is to bake the crust without overcooking the filling. This is why directions call for baking from the frozen state.

Usually crusts will bake and the filling reach the boiling point in about 45-55 minutes, provided a pre-heated oven is used at 425°F.

In what part of the oven would you place a frozen pie if the bottom crust is not browning sufficiently before the top crust is done?

Yes, the fruit will become mushy and lose its identity.

45. Can a fruit filling be damaged by overcooking?

Obviously the colder pie takes longer to heat and bake. Best temperatures to hold frozen pies are zero to +5°F.

46. The temperature of the frozen pie determines in part the necessary time for cooking or baking it.

Which pie takes longer to bake, one held at zero degrees or one at -15°F.?

Not recommended because the crust may burn before the pie is done. Store frozen pies in the freezer, not the refrigerator.

47. How about thawing out a frozen pie before baking it?

Yes, each pie
requires a cer-
tain number of
BTU's to bake.
The oven is
limited in the
number of
BTU's it can
generate.

48. Frozen pumpkin pies may require 10-15 minutes longer to bake than fruit pies. The added time
dries excess moisture and allows the filling to set.

Is more time needed for baking an oven full of
pies than for one or a few pies?

tough and
solid

49. In the chart on the next page, we see that
many things can go wrong in making a pie crust.

If we put in excessive water, the crust will
shrink up and be _____.

liquid.

50. A crumbly pie may be caused by overmixing
of the dough, excessive shortening or from in-
sufficient_____.

wet.

51. If a pie crust sticks to the pan, it may be because of insufficient shortening in the dough, the
fact that some of the filling boiled over and
sticks to the bottom of the pan, not enough bottom heat or the fact that the pie plates were
_____

ORDINARY PIE FAULTS AND THEIR CAUSES

CAUSES / FAULTS	OVER MIXED	INSUFFICIENT SHORTENING	TOO MUCH SHORTENING	IMPROPERLY MIXED	INSUFFICIENT LIQUID	TOO MUCH LIQUID	IMPROPER FLOUR	OVER WORKING OF DOUGH	BAKING TEMP. TOO LOW	BAKING TEMP. TOO HIGH	NO BOTTOM OVEN HEAT	EXCESS ACIDITY IN FILLING	HOT FILLING TOP CRUST	LACK OF OPENING TOP CRUST	IMPROPERLY SEALED CRUSTS	FILLING TOO THIN	WET PIE PLATES	BOILING OVER OF FILLING	TOO MUCH SUGAR	INSUFFICIENT SUGAR	WATERY EGG WHITES	NOT BEAT FIRM ENOUGH
PIE DOUGH																						
STIFF	X				X		X															
CRUMBLY		X	X		X		X															
TOUGH	X	X				X	X	X														
(BAKED CRUST)																						
TOO LIGHT IN COLOR									X		X											
SOLID CRUST						X		X	X													
SHRINKAGE				X				X														
TOUGH	X	X				X	X	X														
(TWO CRUST PIES)																						
UNBAKED CRUST BOTTOM										X	X						X					
BOILING OF FILLING DURING BAKING												X	X	X	X							
CRUST STICKING TO PANS																	X	X	X			
CRUST SOAK ON BOTTOM											X					X	X					
(MERINGUE)																						
WATERY OR WEEPING																			X	X	X	X
TOUGH																				X	X	X

Reprinted with permission of the publisher from J. Amendola's The Baker's Manual for Quantity Baking and Pastry Making, 2nd Edition. Copyright 1956 and 1960 by Ahrens Publishing Company, Inc.

REVIEW

1. A short crust is one that is high in _____ .

2. A chiffon pie has some leavening taking place because of the presence of what ingredient?

3. Soft pie should have <u>flaky/mealy</u> bottom crust.

4. The more shortening in a crust, the <u>more/less</u> tender it is.

5. True or False: A flaky crust always has more shortening in it than a mealy crust.

6. A pie crust which shrinks away from the pan when baked is likely to have <u>too much/too little</u> gluten in it.

7. A principal reason for using ice water in mixing pie dough is to <u>retard/increase</u> gluten development.

8. True or False: To get a flaky crust, it is necessary to hand mix the dough.

9. At about what temperature should the shortening be for mixing into pie dough?

10. What ingredient in dough soaks up most of the water in mixing?

11. Dough which has been thoroughly mixed would be preferably used for which crust, the top or the bottom?

12. True or False: Always use shiny pie tins for baking pies.

13. The purpose of "double panning" of pies is to _____ .

14. Ordinarily, what type of starch is used for thickening a cream or lemon pie?

15. Which starch is better for any filling which will be frozen, regular cornstarch or waxy maize?

16. Cross-linked starches are more/less stable than those that have not been modified.

17. When a starch and water solution is heated and the starch granules absorb much of the water, the process is known as _____.

18. Which of these starches, regular cornstarch or waxy maize, has two thickening periods when it is cooked and cooled?

19. If a starch is overcooked, the resulting solution is thicker/thinner than usual.

20. Too much sugar or the presence of acid interferes with/encourages gelatinization.

21. Weeping in a pie may mean that the filling has been undercooked/overcooked.

Cake Baking

However inspired, no written definition of the word cake could approximate the glories of sweetened dough, baked, filled, frosted, and made ravishing with edible decorations. Such creations can bring happiness to both our childhood and mature years, for few, if any, people are immune to their charm, and memories of them will lighten the dark corners of life.

The word "cake" comes to us from Middle English, and may have had earlier origins in Old Norse. From the earliest days of civilization, man has always considered cake a food for the gods as well as for himself. The Egyptians made cakes in animal, bird, and human forms for their various gods. Greeks offered honey cakes to their gods, and in the North honey cakes were offered to Thor at the winter solstice to ensure a fruitful year to come.

Few pleasures are greater than turning out a perfect cake. And perfect cakes can be achieved by any cook who is careful and who is willing to follow recipe directions. Cake-making is an exact process; the ingredients and their relation to each other are balanced like a chemical formula; in fact, during the baking, a chemical process takes place, transforming the raw ingredients into a delicious new entity.

There are two main classifications of cakes in American fare, those made with fat and those made without.

CAKE MAKING

Careful weighing of the ingredients is absolutely essential to obtain uniform results in cake making. Every bake shop must provide a suitable scale, equipped to weigh from fractions of ounces up to several pounds, to permit accurate scaling of ingredients, particularly leavening agents and flavors. Accurate scaling prevents the products from fluctuating from day to day.

MIXING

The mixing procedure plays a very important part in good cake making and extreme care should be taken in the handling and mixing of the cake batter. Each type of cake batter should be mixed in accordance with a specific formula and every phase of the mixing methods carefully observed.

There are three primary ways to mix cake batters:
(1) Creaming method
(2) Two stage method
(3) Sponge or foam type

CREAMING METHOD
(a) Scale all ingredients carefully and keep all of them at room temperature.
(b) Sugar, shortening or butter, salt, flavors and spices are generally creamed together.
(c) Add required amount of eggs gradually in several small portions and continue to cream.
(d) Next add liquids, milk or water as directed, gradually and carefully. It is advisable to add only a portion of the milk alternately with the flour in some batters.
(e) Add sifted baking powder and flour and mix until a smooth mixture is obtained.

Throughout the entire mixing process the sides of the bowl should be scraped down occasionally to insure a uniform batter.

TWO STAGE METHOD
(a) Scale all ingredients carefully and have all at room temperature.
(b) Place all dry ingredients, such as flour, sugar, spices, baking powder, salt and any other dry ingredients, in mixing bowl, along with the shortening, add part of the milk and mix at a slow speed for required amount of time.
(c) Take the balance of the milk, beat slightly with the required amount of egg, then add this to the above mixture in approximately three parts, scraping the sides of the bowl at intervals while doing so to insure a smooth batter.

SPONGE OR FOAM TYPE MIX
(a) Scale all ingredients carefully and have all at room temperature.
(b) Take eggs and sugar and warm to approximately $100^{\circ}F.$, this is done to dissolve the sugar, then continue to beat until the maximum point is reached.
(c) Fold in flour just enough to insure uniformity.

As we mentioned before, there are variations to these basic methods and every formula for cake making should include complete mixing methods.

CAKE MIXES
These are, and will be increasingly, important, as there will be more and more of this type of product on the market. Mixes eliminate the weighing of ingredients and reduce time and a large part of the work involved in cake making.

CAKE INGREDIENTS AND THEIR FUNCTIONS

MAIN FUNCTIONS IN FINISHED PRODUCTS / INGREDIENTS	MILK	LEAVENING AGENT	FLAVOR & SPICES	EGG WHITES	EGGS WHOLE–YOLKS	SALT	SHORTENING & BUTTER	SUGAR	CAKE FLOUR
BINDING AGENT									X
ABSORBING AGENT									X
AIDS KEEPING QUALITIES	X						X	X	X
AFFECTS EATING QUALITIES									X
NUTRITIONAL VALUE	X				X		X	X	X
AFFECTS FLAVOR					X	X			X
ADDS SWEETNESS								X	
PRODUCES TENDERNESS								X	
AFFECTS SYMMETRY		X						X	
IMPARTS CRUST COLOR							X		
SHORTNESS OR TENDERNESS							X		
EATING QUALITIES							X		
COLOR		X	X						
VOLUME			X	X					
STRUCTURE	X	X	X						
GRAIN AND TEXTURE	X	X					X		
ADDS QUALITY TO PRODUCT	X		X			X			
BRINGS OUT FLAVOR									

Reprinted with permission of the publisher from J. Amendola's The Baker's Manual for Quantity Baking and Pastry Making, 2nd Edition. Copyright 1956 and 1960 by Ahrens Publishing Company, Inc.

ORDINARY CAKE FAULTS AND THEIR CAUSES

CAUSES \ FAULTS	IMPROPER MIXING	BATTER TOO STIFF	TOO MUCH LEAVENING AGENT	NOT ENOUGH LEAVENING AG'T.	BATTER TOO SLACK	TOO MUCH HEAT	NOT ENOUGH HEAT	EXCESSIVE SUGAR	NOT ENOUGH SUGAR	IMPROPER TYPE OF FLOUR	TOO MUCH FLOUR	NOT ENOUGH FLOUR	CAKES SCALED TOO LIGHT	AGED BAKING POWDER	OVER BAKING	UNDER BAKING	SUGAR TOO COARSE	NOT ENOUGH EGGS	FRUIT NOT DRAINED RIGHT	NOT ENOUGH SHORTENING	UNBALANCED FORMULA	BATTER TOO WARM	NOT ENOUGH LIQUID
(EXTERNAL)																							
CRUST TOO DARK							X																
CAKES TOO SMALL				X		X						X								X			X
SPECKS ON CAKE	X																X						
SHRINKAGE OF CAKES	X	X				X																	
CAKE FALLS DURING BAKING	X	X										X											
CAKES BURST ON TOP	X					X		X			X												
CRUST TOO THICK									X														
(INTERNAL)																							
COARSE AND IRREGULAR GRAIN	X	X	X		X		X	X							X					X		X	
DENSE GRAIN					X						X											X	
POOR FLAVOR			X		X													X					X
CAKE TOUGH							X	X												X		X	X
LACK OF BODY IN QUALITY		X	X				X	X								X				X		X	X
SINKING OF FRUIT		X	X					X											X			X	
POOR KEEPING QUALITIES					X		X	X												X		X	

Reprinted with permission of the publisher from J. Amendola's The Baker's Manual for Quantity Baking and Pastry Making, 2nd Edition. Copyright 1956 and 1960 by Ahrens Publishing Company, Inc.

1. What is a cake? The ancient Romans served a kind of cake at their wedding meals, a sweetened white bread. Today, we think of a cake as a baked product made using cake flour (made from soft wheat and relatively low in protein), water and <u>much</u> sugar. The batter made from this mixture usually has eggs, some shortening and leavening, salt and flavoring and perhaps milk powder added to it.

Baking powder is usually added as a leavening agent.

Is a griddle cake a cake?

Not according to our definition. It has very little sugar.

2. Is coffee cake a cake?

Not exactly. It is yeast leavened and is usually made with little or no cake flour. A "sweet dough".

3. A cake is a tender product. Tenderness results partly from the use of cake flour but chiefly from the addition of shortening and sugar.

The use of an oil (or liquid shortening) makes for a more tender cake than the use of a plastic fat. Can you guess why?

When the cake cools the plastic fat tends to firm. It is not quite as tender as when oil is used.

4. Emulsifier-type shortenings give results superior to other fats in cake baking. These hydrogenated fats include mono- and diglycerides added to give spread to the fat in the batter. The mono- and diglycerides increase the emulsifying property of the fat in the cake batter which produces larger volume, finer grain, improved texture and tenderness.

Emulsifiers in cake shortenings have what effect?

They spread the shortening out into finer globules giving a smoother batter and improved texture. Higher ratios of fat and sugar can also be used.

No. It is relatively hard to slice an angel cake, but the cake is still tender enough to eat because of the egg.

5. The reason shortening tenderizes the cake is that the fat or oil surrounds the gluten strands and "shortens" or untoughens them. The shortening produces a "short break", which means that the crumb breaks clean and does not have to be cut or sheared as when gluten strands are present.

An angel cake contains no fat whatsoever. Would you expect the crumb to have a short break (break sharply and easily)?

baking powder

6. Cakes can be classified into:
   1. Fat type cakes
      a. pound
      b. layer
      c. cup
      d. sheet

   2. Foam type cakes
      a. angel
      b. chiffon
      c. sponge
      d. California cheese cake

Fat type cakes usually include baking powder as a leavening agent.

Foam type cakes do not include baking powder. Leavening is achieved by the air whipped into the eggs used.

Fat type cakes include_____;
foam types do not.

False. Only
part of the
leavening is a
result of the
CO_2 formed by
the baking
powder.

7. Fat type cakes are developed from batter which is of the oil-in-water type attained by proper mixing. Creamed into the center of each droplet of fat or oil is a tiny air cell which acts as a nucleus to pick up leavening gases when loosed in the oven by the heat. These cells further expand by as much as 80% when joined by water vapors formed by the heat of the oven.

In the case of pound cakes enough air volume is initially creamed in so that no baking powder at all is necessary. It is expanded totally by oven-generated water vapor. However, most commercial pound cakes, because they are "leaner" in composition (less fat and eggs), utilize a boost from a greatly reduced "dose" of baking powder.

True or False: Fat type cakes rely completely on baking powder for their leavening action.

More

8. Rules governing the formulation of fat type cakes are simple:
   1. The sugar should exceed the flour.
   2. The liquid (combined water or liquid milk) and eggs should exceed the sugar.
   3. The eggs should exceed the shortening.

Fat type cakes—pound, layer, cup and sheet—include shortening, sugar and eggs. They should include more/less sugar than flour.

More

9. Fat type cakes include more/less eggs than shortening.

More

10. In fat-type cakes there should be more/less liquid than sugar.

No. The flour is not "strong enough" to support the yeast action. There is not enough gluten to contain the vigorous gas formation from the yeast.

11. Cakes are made using cake flour made from a soft wheat and relatively low in protein. Can cake flour be leavened by yeast action?

eggs

12. Leavening action in cakes results from creaming fat and sugar together, from baking powder action or from air trapped in beaten _____.

Air

13. Cakes rise because gases in the batter expand when heated. The enlarged bubbles stretch the protein present. During baking the heat sets the protein and we have a large volume cake. What gas is involved in the leavening of angel cakes and pound cakes?

Carbon dioxide

14. In chemically leavened cakes, what gas beside air is involved?

increase

15. The volume of many cakes depends largely upon the volume obtained in creaming the shortening, sugar and eggs. Use shortening which produces good creaming volume. For maximum creaming quality, the shortening should be at about 75°F. Higher temperatures reduce creaming quality. Batter temperatures should be 70°F. ± 2°F.

Two parts of sugar to one part of shortening results in maximum creaming volume.

Fine granulated sugar is best.

Creaming should be done at lower speeds unless the temperature of the fat is below 70°F. Using a higher speed heats up the fat.

It sometimes takes 8-10 minutes to incorporate the maximum amount of air.

A major purpose of creaming is to_____ the volume of the cake.

8-10

16. The creaming process may take as long as____ minutes to attain maximum volume.

more

17. Unless the percentage of shortening and eggs is high, one ounce of baking powder to each pound of flour is used. It stands to reason that if a cake formula is low in shortening and eggs, more/less leavening agent will be needed.

The bowl must be large enough to allow maximum incorporation of air. About 3½ pounds of eggs and sugar require a bowl of 10 quart capacity.

18. In mixing eggs and sugar do you think the size of the bowl has any connection with amount of creaming action?

The protein filaments are stretched very thinly. Even so, extreme care must be exercised in making angel food cake to prevent its becoming tough.

19. Another way of classifying cakes is according to the amount of fat contained in the cake. The old fashioned pound cake is the richest in fat, containing 80 pounds of fat to 100 pounds of flour.

The angel food cake on the other hand contains no fat at all.

Without fat how can the angel cake be tender?

Yes

20. The old fashioned sponge cake contained no added fat and for this reason dried out quickly. Sponge cake contains some fat because whole eggs are used and egg yolks contain about 1/3 fat.

Would you develop tenderness in a sponge cake by adding some fat?

No, for the
same reason
that angel and
sponge cakes
pans are not
greased.

21. Chiffon cakes are leavened by beaten eggs and some baking powder. They contain oil instead of fat. The large quantity of beaten eggs used gives them the characteristic of sponge cakes. The beaten eggs are folded into the batter at the end of the mixing period so that the eggs will attain volume for leavening.

Would you grease the pans used for baking chiffon cakes?

beaten eggs

22. Cakes can be divided into those that depend upon <u>creaming</u>, those that depend on <u>baking powder</u>, and those that depend upon_____
for their lightness.

tough

23. The precise baker uses different flours for different cakes. The heavy pound cake can use a fairly strong cake flour to advantage.

Cakes leavened with baking powder require flour not quite as strong.

Cakes leavened with beaten eggs use a very soft flour.

If a strong flour were used in a sponge or angel cake, would the cake tend to be tough or tender?

24. Cakes fail, i.e. do not achieve their optimal size, appearance and texture for a number of reasons. Obviously if the formula is incorrect, if there is too much baking powder, too much sugar, or too much or too little of any ingredient, the cake will <u>fail</u>. Excessive baking powder, for example, produces a cake with a coarse grain which dries out rapidly. A pocket in the bottom of the cake forms if there is too much milk. The flour may be too strong or too weak for the cake desired. A cake will peak in the center if there is too little baking powder or too many eggs or too high a bottom (oven) heat. Too little liquid will cause it to "dip".

improper
creaming and
improper heat
control

Aside from an improper formula, the two principal reasons for failures other than the wrong quantities of ingredients are the mixing procedure and the control of the heat in the oven.

Three principal reasons for cake failures are improper amount of ingredients,_____ and_____.

25. If too much air is incorporated into the batter, the cake may dip in the center. The grain is very compact, the cells small.

the oven being
too hot

A baked cake may peak in the center if too many eggs or too much milk is used or if there is not enough sugar or baking powder.

Another reason for cake peaking in the center is that the oven has been too hot. Check the bottom of the cake to see if it is overly brown.

Cakes that peak in the center can either have the wrong ingredients in them or the peaking can have been caused by_____.

26. Cakes can be too tender, falling apart when they are picked up. This can be caused by too much baking powder, sugar or not enough eggs, or because of improper mixing.

overly tender

Another reason for excessively tender cakes is that the oven temperature has been too low.

If a cake has too much fat or sugar or if the oven temperature has been too low the cake is likely to be_____.

shrink

27. Another reason for cake failure is shrinkage, the cake pulls away from the sides of the pan and drops.

Shrinkage can be caused by using too much milk (water) or fat. Another reason for shrinkage is that the oven is too hot. An excessively hot oven causes cracks on the top and a dark bottom crust.

If the oven temperature is too high the cake is likely to crack on the top, be overly browned on the bottom and_____.

little or no

28. Some ingredients are thought of as tougheners, others as tenderizers. Flour and eggs are structure builders and tougheners. Shortening and sugar are tenderizers.

Judging from the above, to get a chewy loaf of bread, you would include much/little or no shortening.

shortening

29. To achieve a tender cake, you would include flour which has developed minimum amount of gluten and include sugar and_____.

Indeed yes. He does not have to be a food chemist, but he should know how to control the leavening action.

30. Most baked items are leavened. A gas such as air, steam or carbon dioxide, expands the dough or batter to produce a larger volume. Doughs are usually expanded by carbon dioxide which is produced by the splitting of the sugar by the yeast present. Cakes are usually leavened by the use of baking powder which releases carbon dioxide when mixed with water and in the presence of heat. Baking soda and an acid also release carbon dioxide to produce leavening.

Should the baker know something about what takes place when a dough, batter or paste is leavened?

Sugar

31. Sugar is added to dough to make sweet doughs. It is added to cakes to add sweetness and to make the crumb more tender. In yeast products some of the sugar serves as food for the yeast. Some of the sugar is split so that part of it becomes carbon dioxide gas which leavens the dough. Most of us think of sugar as being only the sucrose we use on the table from cane or sugar beets. But there are other sugars. Sucrose itself can be split (hydrolized) into simpler forms of sugar known as glucose and fructose. Sugars vary in the degree of sweetness that we experience when we eat them. Some sugars, especially those high in invert sugar, hold water better than others; honey, for example.

What ingredient in baked products is split to form carbon dioxide and alcohol?

THE MECHANICS OF CAKE BAKING

Excessive gluten is developed and bready texture results.

32. The mechanics of mixing a cake are important to the final product. If the batter is beaten too long, what will happen to the cake?

The cake needs to cling to the sides of the pan for support.

33. Only the bottoms of cake pans are greased and for a very good reason. The ungreased sides permit the cake to cling to the sides thereby reducing the chances of the cake falling. The baker's brush is usually used to grease the bottom of the pan.

In baking sheet cakes, fill the pan only half or not more than 2/3 full.

Why not grease the sides of the cake pan?

No, each time the door is opened the temperature drops sharply

34. Cakes are done when they spring back when touched lightly or when they have pulled away from the sides of the pan. The volume of the cake and the color of the top of the cake are also indicators of doneness.

Is it a good idea to open the oven door from time to time to check on the doneness of the cake?

The dull iron one absorbs and transmits heat faster and more effectively than the pans having a shiny surface. Dull pans result in faster browning.

35. Fast heat penetration is desired in cake baking. What kind of metal pan would be best for baking cake: one made of iron with a dull finish or a bright aluminum pan?

Yes, allow free air circulation around the pans. If they touch each other or the sides of the oven, the rate of heat transfer is increased where they touch.

36. Is it reasonable to suggest that when placing cakes in an oven the pans be placed so that they do not touch the sides of the oven or are located directly over one another?

Yes, it is recommended that cakes be allowed to cool to 140°F. This may take a long time. At least let them cool for 10 to 15 minutes so that their centers will be partially cooled.

37. Knowing that a warm, freshly baked cake breaks easily if handled, would it be wise to allow the cake to cool before removing from the pan?

True, because of the proportionately smaller surface exposure.

38. A sheet cake, baked as a large unit, retains its moisture and freshness longer than if the same amount of cake were made in smaller units. The smaller units have proportionately more surface area exposed to the air. The sheets can be baked and stored, then cut into a variety of squares, bars and other shapes.

True or False: Sheet cakes are less likely to dry out than smaller sized cakes.

REVIEW

1. Cake is a flour and water mixture that always contains much of what other ingredient?

2. While bread products are leavened by the use of yeast, most cakes are leavened by the use of _____.

3. Angel food cake has no leavening agent added to it; leavening is effected by the action of _____.

4. Which type of cake—fat type or foam type—uses baking powder as a leavening agent?

5. In cakes, sugar exceeds/is less than the quantity of flour.

6. What would happen to a cake if it were leavened by yeast action?

7. When fat and sugar are creamed together, air is incorporated into the mixture. What happens to this air when the product is baked?

8. If we use a high speed for creaming sugar and fat, what is likely to happen?

9. At what temperature should sugar and fat be for best creaming action?

10. For maximum creaming volume, we want one part of shortening to _____ parts of sugar.

11. Ordinarily, in a cake formula, one pound of baking powder is used to _____ pounds of flour.

12. Which two ingredients used in baking are tougheners and structure builders?

13. Flour is also a bulk builder. What is another bulk builder in baking?

14. Certain bakery ingredients are thought of as tenderizing agents. These are sugar, shortening, and the _____ agent.

15. Only one bakery ingredient is thought of as being a lubricant. This is _____ .

16. Give an example of a flour and water mixture that is a paste.

17. What type of flour—all purpose, pastry or bread—is likely to be found in the home?

18. Shortening is fat used in baking which has what effect on the gluten?

19. In using bakers' percentages, the formula is always computed as a percentage of the weight of what ingredient?

20. How much shortening is used in an Angel Food Cake?

21. Cakes get their volume and lightness with the action of baking powder, creaming, or the use of _____ .

22. What type of flour would you want to use for a sponge cake?

23. A pound cake, the richest in fat, would need a stronger/weaker flour than a foam type cake.

24. If a cake peaks in the center when baking, it may be caused by too little baking powder, too many eggs, or _____ .

25. What will cause a cake to dip in the middle?

26. If excessive baking powder is used, the cake will have a coarse/fine grain and will dry out rapidly.

27. If too much air is incorpoarted into the batter of a baked cake, it will peak/dip in the center.

28. A baked cake may peak in the center if there is too much/too little baking powder.

29. Some of the reasons for an excessively tender cake are that the oven temperature is too low, or that it contains too much fat or _____.

30. Cake that is cracked on the top, brown on the bottom, and shrinks away from the pan, has likely been cooked in an oven that is _____.

31. Overmixing of a batter will develop too much gluten which results in a tender/tough cake.

32. Baking powder releases carbon dioxide when mixed with water and in the presence of an alkali/acid.

33. To get a moist cake, we might include what type of sugar?

34. When baking, a cake forms a new, larger structure, supported by gelatinized starch and _____.

35. The recipe for chiffon cake calls for a hydrogenated shortening/oil.

36. The tube in the middle of an angel food cake pan serves to pass heat quickly into the batter and to _____.

37. Cake should be allowed to cool before handling; otherwise it is likely to _____.

38. What happens to a cake which is mixed too long?

CAKE FROSTINGS, FILLINGS AND GLAZES

These are sweet decorative coatings placed between layers or over the tops and sides of the cake to add to the flavor and appearance.

FROSTING—Frosting or icing means the same thing. Frostings are both cooked and uncooked.

Cooked frostings, such as White Mountain Frosting, are made by beating a hot sugar syrup into beaten egg whites. Another method is to cook sugar, butter, and liquid into a candylike frosting such as in Fudge Frosting.

Uncooked frostings, such as Butter Frosting, are made by beating together butter, some liquid, flavoring and confectioners' sugar. Decorators' Frosting is made by beating egg whites with confectioners' sugar.

FILLING—Cooked fillings include liquid or fruit thickened with cornstarch, egg, or flour, such as Cream Filling or Pineapple Filling.

Uncooked fillings include those made with whipped cream, chopped fruit, jelly, or instant pudding.

GLAZE—A glaze is a thin glossy coating with a firm consistency. It can be cooked or uncooked. Some are baked or broiled onto cakes, others are spread on hot cakes.

Attractive icings promote the sale of cakes. They have other important functions:
(1) Icings improve the keeping quality of cakes.
(2) Icings form a protective coating around the cake trapping in the moisture.
(3) Icings help improve the taste of the cake and make a most attractive item for sales and eye appeal.

Proper combinations of flavor are imperative. Use only the very best quality of flavoring. There is no saving in poor or cheap flavoring, as it destroys the quality of the entire product.

Use fresh fruit when obtainable for fruit icings.

Be careful not to use food colors in too lavish a manner since it will result in dark icings which are not attractive. Delicate pastel colorings enhance the eye appeal of the icing, too much color destroys the product. Study color combinations carefully and test them out for delicacy. Err on the side of too pale rather than too heavy coloring.

There are seven basic icings:
- (1) Fondant
- (2) Buttercream
- (3) Fudge
- (4) Flat
- (5) Boiled
- (6) Marshmallow
- (7) Royal

Fondant icing is a syrup of glucose, sugar and water cooked to 240°F., then cooled to approximately 110°F. and worked quickly until it is creamy, white and smooth.

This is a somewhat difficult icing to make and when required in quantity it has become customary to purchase a uniform fondant icing from your baker's supply house. Store the prepared fondant in containers, covering them with a damp cloth or with a small amount of water over the icing to prevent drying out of the fondant.

When ready to use the fondant icing, take the desired quantity and heat it over a warm bath, stirring constantly, to blood heat—98°F. to 100°F. This process will thin down the icing and cause it to flow freely.

If the icing is still heavy, a simple syrup may be used to thin it a little more. Fondant icing may be flavored or colored as desired and is used primarily for pouring and dipping.

Do not heat fondant icing above 100°F. It will lose its glossiness and create a dull finish for the product. Fondant may be used as a base for other icings, i.e. Buttercream, by creaming the butter or shortening with the fondant to create fluffier icings.

Buttercream is made by creaming the icing sugar, butter or shortening, and eggs which are added to give the icing the desired consistency. The amount of creaming depends upon the lightness required in the finished product. Buttercream may be colored and flavored as desired. When not in use, store this icing in a cool place with a wax paper covering. Buttercream is generally used for layer cakes, decorated cakes, etc.

Fudge icing requires the cooking of the sugar into a syrup in order to obtain the smoothness required in the finished icing. When the hot syrup is added to the balance of the ingredients in the formula, it creates a rather heavy body. Before applying the icing to the cake, fudge icing should be heated slightly in a water bath. When fudge icing is not in use it should be properly stored and covered to prevent spoilage and drying. Fudge icing is generally used on cup cakes and layer cakes.

Flat icing or Plain water icing. This is a simple icing. Mix well all basic ingredients—water, icing sugar, corn syrup and flavor. Before applying flat icing to coffee cake, danish cake, etc. heat it to 100°F. and apply by hand or pastry brush to the product. Flat icing is usually white and flavored with vanilla or lemon. Coloring may be used, but very sparing-

116

ly if at all. Store icing properly when not in use and be sure to keep it covered.

Boiled icing. Cook a syrup of sugar, water and glucose. Add to beaten eggs while hot. Heavier syrup produces a heavier icing. Thinner icing is produced by thinner syrup. This icing should be applied generously and left in peaks on the cake. Boiled icing breaks down if stored overnight and should be made only in needed amounts each time.

Marshmallow icing is a variation of boiled icing but has a stabilizer, usually gelatin and confectioners' sugar, added to it. It is applied in the same manner as boiled icing.

Royal or Decorating icing is a fairly simple icing to make. Beat together icing sugar, egg whites and an acid agent, until a smooth consistency is obtained. Royal icing is used primarily for decorating and flower making. It is often used to make cake 'dummies'. It is seldom used on stable cakes as it tends to become hard and brittle. Royal icing can be colored as desired and should be covered with a damp cloth when not in use.

CAKE ICINGS

To enhance appearance, to extend shelf life, and to increase the flavor.

1. Cakes are coated with frostings or icings to enhance appearance, to extend the shelf life by forming a protective coating and to hold in the moisture and increase the flavor of the cake.

Frostings or icings are divided into those which are cooked and those uncooked. A butter cream frosting, for example, is made by merely beating together butter (shortening), some liquid flavoring, and confectioners (powdered) sugar of the ultra-fine type (confectioners 10X).

Why should we coat cakes with frosting?

Confectioners sugar is ground into tiny particle size and will not be tasted as granular (will not be gritty).

2. Decorator's frosting is made by beating egg whites with confectioners sugar.

Why confectioners sugar?

3. Fondant icing is a syrup of glucose, granulated sugar and water cooked at 240°F., and then cooled to about 110°F. and worked quickly until it is creamy, white and smooth.

The rate of formation of the sugar crystals in the fondant determines whether or not the fondant is smooth and free of a gritty or a grainy texture (large sugar crystals).

A fondant is a creamy, granulated sugar, glucose and water mixture in which the sugar crystals are tiny/large.

Most of the larger shops do because of the time involved in making fondant and the possibility of large sugar crystals forming in it if made in the shop.

4. Fondant can be purchased already made.

Would it be wise for the bakeshop to purchase prepared fondant?

It holds in the moisture and extends the shelf life of the cake.

5. Icings can be divided into those that are cooked and those that are uncooked. Fondants, fudges, boiled and marshmallow icings are cooked.

Butter creams, flat or plain water icings and royal and decorating icings are uncooked.

The simplest icing is flat or plain icing which is merely a mixture of water and sugar, corn syrup and flavoring. It is heated to 100°F. so that the sugar goes into solution and the icing can be applied by hand or with a pastry brush.

Royal or decorating icing is used primarily for decorating and flower making. It tends to become hard and brittle.

All icings are basically sugar and water, and sometimes egg whites. Butter cream is the only icing to which an appreciable amount of fat is added.

Icings are applied to cake to add flavor and enhance the appearance. What other important function does an icing perform for a cake?

Yes, the frost-
ing helps to
keep the cake
from drying
out.

6. Frostings, icings, and glazes are sugar and water mixtures, some of which have egg whites added
to them. The purpose of these coatings is to add
flavor, enhance the appearance, and help hold in
the moisture of the cake.

Would you expect a frosted cake to be more
moist than an unfrosted one?

glucose (a
form of sugar)

7. In some types of boiled icings, gelatin and egg
whites are added to impart body and structure to
the icing.

Glucose, invert sugar and malt syrup are also
sometimes added because they are moisture retaining agents which aid in keeping the icing soft and
fresh. Another reason for adding invert sugar is
that it interferes with the formation of large sugar
crystals, resulting in a smoother icing.

To keep an icing moist, malt syrup, invert sugar or_____may be added.

dried milk

8. In damp weather icings which ordinarily
would have a dry surface may become sticky. To
overcome this, a small amount of flour or other
drying agents, such as dried milk or gelatin, are
added.

Sometimes moisture retaining ingredients are
added to a boiled icing; at other times drying agents
such as flour, gelatin or_____may be added.

Shortening,
5-25% of the
amount of sugar used.

9. To get a soft, glossy surface on the icing, from 5-25% of the amount of sugar used in the icing may be added in the form of shortening. The fat particles help disperse the tiny sugar crystals and produce a smooth, light icing.

Various ingredients are added to icings for particular purposes. Gelatin and egg whites give the icing more body. Glucose, invert sugar and malt syrup keep the icing moist. To dry out icing, flour and dried milk and gelatin may be added.

What is likely to be added to make a very smooth, flat icing?

The air that has
been whipped
into the mixture
makes it lighter
and fluffier.

10. Creamed icings made by whipping air into fat and sugar give the icing considerable bulk and increase the volume of the cake. Adding beaten eggs also increases the volume and the foamy character of the icing.

What is it that gives a creamed icing its volume?

sucrose

11. A further word about the sugars used in baking, especially those used in icings.

The usual household sugar is sucrose made from beets or sugar cane.

Molasses is also sucrose but it contains 20-25% water, 2-5% mineral matter and 15-30% invert sugar.

Invert sugar occurs naturally in honey and molasses and it can be made by the action of an acid or an enzyme, invertose, acting on sucrose.

The usual granulated sugar that is used in the bakeshop is_____ .

12. Invert sugar, relatively new to the bakeshop, has certain advantages over sucrose, the ordinary granulated sugar. It has a remarkable ability to hold or retain moisture. Because of this fact it delays the staling of cake or other baked goods which have a tendency to dry out too rapidly.

Invert sugar helps prevent the formation of large sugar crystals which are experienced as graininess. In this way it promotes a desirable smoothness in many icings.

Invert sugar is sweeter to the taste than sucrose.

Invert sugar helps produce a rich brown color on the crust of baked products.

Invert sugar used in icings prolongs the freshness, adds smoothness and is just as <u>sweet as/sweeter</u> than sucrose.

13. Commercial glucose, more commonly known as corn syrup, also has the ability to hold moisture and helps produce a glossy surface on the icing. Like invert sugar, commercial glucose also prevents formation of large crystals of sugar and graininess.

The addition of shortening, egg whites, or invert sugar to a sugar-water mixture interferes with the formation of large sugar crystals and prevents graininess. What other sugar will do the same thing?

REVIEW

1. Volume in an icing is created by the _____ action.

2. Besides adding invert sugar to an icing to produce a smooth light icing, what other ingredient might be added?

3. Fondant icing is a cooked/uncooked icing.

4. A butter cream frosting is cooked/uncooked.

5. Fondant icing is cooked/uncooked.

6. A fondant icing tastes gritty or smooth depending upon the _____.

7. Flat or plain icing is a mixture of water, sugar, flavoring and _____ _____.

8. What type of sugar would be added to an icing recipe to help retain the moisture in the icing?

9. Invert sugar, besides retaining moisture, helps produce a smooth/coarse icing.

10. Which is sweeter: invert sugar or sucrose?

Cookies

At one time, what we now call a cookie was referred to as a small cake or sweet biscuit. We must thank the Dutch for providing us with a special name for it. It is derived from Koekje or Koekie, meaning a "small cake". The word "cookie" is an American usage; in England what we know as cookies are called biscuits.

There are more varieties of cookies than of any other baked product because there are so many different shapes, sizes, textures and flavorings possible. To the basic ingredients, often the same as those used in cakes, all kinds of flavorings may be added: extracts, spices, nuts and fruits. Decorations of every sort are always in order.

Cookies are usually classified according to the way in which the dough is shaped. The six classifications are: 1) bars and squares, 2) drop cookies, 3) rolled cookies, 4) pressed cookies, 5) molded or shaped cookies, and 6) refrigerator cookies. Bar and drop cookies are made with soft dough which has a comparatively high percentage of liquid. The other varieties call for stiff dough, usually less sweet and often higher in fat content than soft dough.

Cookies are one of the most profitable items produced by bakers. A most important factor in their production is the use of high grade ingredients. Butter is the preferred shortening in making cookies. Careful selection of the purest of spices, molasses and flavorings will assure delicious cookies.

Cookies should be baked fresh daily if possible. When it is found necessary to bake ahead, a week's output can be prepared in advance and properly stored.

COOKIE MIXING METHODS
(1) THE ONE STAGE METHOD
   (a) Place all the ingredients into a mixing bowl and mix until all are smoothly blended.
   (b) Allow two or three minutes at low speed for the mixing.

(2) CREAMING METHOD
   (a) Place sugar, shortening or butter, salt and spices in the mixing bowl and cream together.
   (b) Add the eggs and liquid.
   (c) Add last the flour and leavening agent.

The following are the six types of cookies:
(1) ROLLED
    (a) Rolled on a flour bag, easier to handle if chilled first.
    (b) Roll out 1/8 inch thick.
    (c) Cut in desired shape and size with a cookie cutter.
    (d) Place on baking sheets and bake.

(2) ICE BOX OR REFRIGERATOR
    (a) Scale dough at 1 lb., 8 oz. and roll into bars 18 inches long.
    (b) Roll onto waxed paper and place rolls on sheet pans.
    (c) Refrigerate overnight.
    (d) Slice into ½ inch strips and bake.

(3) SPRITZ OR BAGGED
    (a) Put mixture into pastry bag with desired size and shape tube.
    (b) Press directly onto sheet pans.
    (c) Garnish with cherries, nuts, etc. and bake.

(4) BAR
    (a) Scale the dough into 1 lb. pieces and roll out to the length of the sheet pan. Place on the sheet pans, leaving a space between the strips.
    (b) Place three strips to the pan.
    (c) Flatten with the fingers and shape into uniform 1-in. strips.
    (d) Egg wash and bake.

(5) SHEET
    (a) Spread the cookie mixture onto sheet pans.
    (b) Wash or sprinkle with nuts and bake.
    (c) Cool and cut into squares or oblongs.

(6) DROPPED
    (a) Drop mixture onto sheet pans with a spoon or by hand.
    (b) Press or flatten out with a weight or special cookie die.
    (c) You can also cut a strip of dough into ½ ounce pieces.
    (d) If the dough is a rich dough it will spread by itself; do not press or flatten.

biscuits

1. At one time, what we now call a cookie was referred to as a small cake or sweet biscuit. We must thank the Dutch for providing us with a special name for it. It is derived from Koekje or Koekie, meaning a "small cake". The word cookie is an American usage; in England what we know as cookies are called biscuits.

In England cookies are called_____.

bars and
squares, drop
cookies, rolled
cookies, pressed
cookies, molded
or shaped cook-
ies, refrigerator
cookies.

2. There are more varieties of cookies than any other baked product because there are so many different shapes, sizes, textures and flavorings possible. To the basic ingredients, often the same as those used in cakes, all kinds of flavorings may be added: extracts, spices, nuts, and fruits. Decorations of every sort are always in order.

Cookies are usually classified according to the way in which the dough is shaped. The six classifications are: 1) bars and squares, 2) drop cookies, 3) rolled cookies, 4) pressed cookies, 5) molded or shaped cookies, and 6) refrigerator cookies. Bar and drop cookies are made with soft dough which has a comparatively high percentage of liquid. The other varieties call for stiff dough, usually less sweet and often higher in fat content than soft dough.

Name six classifications of cookies.

Butter

3. Cookies are one of the most profitable items produced by bakers. A most important factor in their production is the use of high grade ingredients. Butter is the preferred shortening in making cookies. Careful selection of the purest of spices, molasses and flavorings will assure delicious cookies.

_____is the preferred shortening in making cookies.

fresh daily

4. Cookies should be baked fresh daily, if possible. When it is found necessary to bake ahead, a week's output can be prepared in advance and properly stored.

If possible, cookies should be baked_____.

ORDINARY COOKIE FAULTS AND THEIR CAUSES

CAUSES \ FAULTS	LACK OF SPREAD	SUGARY CRUST	STICKING TO PANS	LACK OF FLAVOR	PALE IN COLOR	DRY	HARD	TOUGH	CRUMBLY	SPREADING
IMPROPER MIX	X	X	X					X	X	X
INSUFFICIENT SUGAR	X				X			X		
TOO MUCH SUGAR		X	X					X	X	X
FLOUR TOO STRONG	X						X	X	X	
TOO MUCH FLOUR						X	X	X		
INSUFFICIENT LEAVENING	X									
TOO MUCH LEAVENING		X			X				X	
TOO MUCH BAKING SODA										X
NOT ENOUGH BAKING SODA	X									
INSUFFICIENT EGGS									X	
TOO MUCH SHORTENING										X
INSUFFICIENT SHORTENING						X	X			
OVER BAKED						X	X			
TOO LOW BAKING TEMPERATURE						X	X	X		X
TOO HIGH BAKING TEMPERATURE	X									
PAN INSUFFICIENTLY GREASED	X		X							
DOUGH TOO SLACK										X
INSUFFICIENT LIQUID						X	X			
POOR QUALITY INGREDIENTS				X						
UNBALANCED FORMULA				X	X					
COOKIE PANS UNCLEAN & UNEVEN			X	X						

REVIEW

1. What do the English call cookies?

2. What are six classifications of cookies?

3. In which classifications is a soft dough used?

4. What is the preferred shortening in making cookies?

5. Name the two cookie mixing methods.

126

Reprinted with permission of the publisher from J. Amendola's The Baker's Manual for Quantity Baking and Pastry Making, 2nd Edition. Copyright 1956 and 1960 by Ahrens Publishing Company, Inc.

Pudding, Creams

The word "pudding" is used to describe a wide variety of baked, boiled or steamed soft foods, either savory or sweet, served hot or cold, as main dishes, side dishes or desserts. Pudding is also another name for blood sausage.

The chief types of puddings are: (1) unsweetened boiled or baked dishes, usually with a cereal base and a texture resembling custard, such as corn pudding; (2) sweetened boiled or baked dishes of a soft, spongy or thick creamy consistency, such as chocolate pudding; and (3) suet-based or suet-custard dishes, such as plum pudding, which were originally boiled in a bag, but are now often baked or steamed.

There seems to be no end to the variety of puddings, both savory and sweet. Puddings have had a long culinary history and there has been time for cooks to develop all sorts of recipes. The name itself may be related to old Germanic words meaning "sausage" or "swollen". Certainly blood puddings such as Haggis, that Scottish conglomeration Robert Burns called the "great chieftain o' the pudding race", are swollen. Also swollen and encased like a sausage are the early English "puddynges" of the 14th century. These were often suet crusted, such as the now popular steak and kidney pudding. Steamed within a bag or cloth in a huge kettle along with the rest of the dinner, they became swollen. The bag or cloth took the place of the sausage casing.

Sweet dessert puddings are relatively modern. It was only when sugar became available in the late 18th and early 19th century that sweet puddings came into their own. The sweet puddings were of such great variety that Englishmen now often use the word to mean dessert.

Americans inherit the English enjoyment of puddings. The early settlers of New England ate their puddings as a first course. It may have well been an Indian pudding, made with the cornmeal the Indians introduced to the colonists. For the early Americans used native ingredients to build upon the foundations of English pudding cookery. Hasty pudding, for instance, was quickly made in England with wheat flour. Here, where wheat flour was not available, the colonists used cornmeal or a mixture known as rye 'n Injun. Sweetened with maple sugar, the New England hasty pudding was and is a delight.

Today, in addition to the almost endless number of puddings to be made from scratch at home, there is available a wide variety of canned puddings and packaged pudding mixes.

Puddings are very popular desserts, economical and profitable. The careful preparation of puddings is imperative to obtain a good result. All too often puddings are prepared haphazardly and this results in a mediocre finished product. As in all good products, method and recipe go hand in hand and an attractive manner of serving the item is also of importance.

There are five basic methods of preparing puddings:
    (1) Boiled
    (2) Baked
    (3) Chilled
    (4) Steamed
    (5) Souffle

The boiled, baked and chilled puddings are the most popular in commercial food operations.

The steamed pudding is generally served during the cold season as it tends to be heavy and is usually served with a hot sauce. This pudding can be served very attractively if care is taken with the final preparation.

The souffle is adaptable to a la carte service. It must be made just before service to secure lightness and fluffiness or it will become heavy and soggy. Thus, one can see that souffles are not a good choice for the cafeteria.

SAUCES FOR PUDDINGS AND ICE CREAMS

There are three basic sauces from which a great many varieties may be made by the addition of various ingredients. These are:

(1) CREAM SAUCE—First and most popular is the cream sauce developed from milk, sugar, eggs or egg yolks and water cooked to a very soft custard, flavored and served either hot or cold.

(2) FRUIT SAUCE—Fruit sauce is made from fruit or fruit juices, boiled with water and flavored. Lemon juice is then added and the whole reduced or thickened, as the case may be, with a small amount of starch, then cooked until it becomes a thin jell like sauce.

(3) HARD SAUCE—Hard sauce consists of powdered sugar and butter creamed lightly, sometimes thinned down with cream or egg and flavored. Hard sauce is always served cold on hot puddings or apple dumplings.

PASTRY CREAMS OR CUSTARD CREAMS

Custard creams, milk custards, cream fillings, etc. must always be carefully made and handled, but precautions are especially important during the summer months. In many instances, alleged food poisoning attributed to various bakery cream products has been detrimental not only to the individual food service operation but has adversely affected all quantity operations.

With the approach of warm weather, increased caution and care must be the watchword in the production and distribution of cream goods. Creams and custards are a perfect media for bacteria contamination and growth.

1.   Don't use wooden or composition containers for mixing or storing cream goods. (Never store in copper containers).

2.   Don't use hands for stirring. Hands must never come in contact with custard cream.

3.   Don't use leftover custard creams.

4.   Don't expose custard to shop dust; keep covered while cooling.

5.   Don't cool slowly as creams become easily contaminated.

6.   Don't use day-old or leftover cream puffs, eclairs or other cream goods.

Many state health departments have passed laws and adopted regulations governing manufacture and sale of bakery goods. Some of these regulations prohibit the sale of cream goods for a definite period during the summer months, others require refrigeration.

Check your state and local food and health laws and protect yourself by definitely following such laws as may be in force. If these laws are difficult to follow, it would be definitely to your advantage to discontinue the sale of cream goods during the extremely hot weather.

1.   It is important that all employees handling cream goods and custards are clean, tidy and careful about their hygeine.

2.   Use only metal containers that have been thoroughly sterilized for preparing and cooking.

3.   Use sterile shallow pans plus refrigeration for quickly cooling custard.

4.   Use sterile wooden spoon or spatula for stirring. Also use sterile filling machine for cream puffs and similar items.

5. Destroy leftover custard cream and day-old or leftover finished products.

6. Just because day-old creams have a pleasant, sweet, palatable taste does not mean that they are satisfactory; the various harmful bacteria do not always impart an unpleasant or distinguishable taste to the product.

7. If you run a take-out operation, educate customers to the fact that cream and custard items are perishable and that refrigeration in the home is necessary.

PASTRY CREAM (CREAM PATISSIERE)

Pastry cream is a cream filling that plays an important part in the making of many desserts. It is one of the basic necessities all students should know how to make and it is very important that it should be made well.

Smoothness and flavor are especially important and, therefore, great care should be taken during the mixing and boiling process. The milk should be boiled with one-half of the sugar. The eggs or egg yolks should be well beaten with the rest of the sugar, flour and cornstarch.

When the milk boils, a part of the milk should be mixed with the egg mixture. Then this milk-egg mixture should be mixed into the boiling milk. These are then boiled together while stirring continuously with a whip to prevent the cream from burning or scorching and at the same time to insure a thorough mixing and to obtain a smooth cream. Add butter and flavor last.

Caution: Never allow your sugar and eggs to stand without mixing. If you do, your sugar will curdle or burn the eggs causing small hard lumps to form. Then you will find it necessary to strain your mixture before using it, thus losing some of the value of the eggs and making the cream grainy instead of smooth.

soft

1. Pudding is used to describe a wide variety of baked, boiled or steamed soft foods, either savory or sweet, served hot or cold, as main dishes, side dishes, or desserts. Pudding is also another name for blood sausage.

Puddings come in a wide variety, but they are all_____.

130

suet-based

2. The chief types of pudding are: unsweetened boiled or baked dishes, usually with a cereal base and a texture resembling custard, such as corn pudding; sweetened boiled or baked dishes of a soft, spongy or thick creamy consistency, such as chocolate pudding; and suet-based or suet-custard dishes, such as plum pudding, which were originally boiled in a bag, but are now often baked or steamed.

Three chief types of puddings are: unsweetened, sweetened, _____.

sugar

3. Sweet dessert puddings are relatively modern. It was only when sugar became widely available in the late 18th and early 19th centuries that sweet puddings came into their own. The sweet puddings were of such great variety that Englishmen now often use the word to mean dessert.

The availability of _____ was responsible for the popularity of sweet puddings.

careful preparation

4. Puddings are very popular desserts, economical and profitable. The careful preparation of puddings is imperative to obtain a good result. All too often puddings are prepared haphazardly and this results in a mediocre finished product. As in all good products, method and recipe go hand in hand and the attractive manner of serving the item is also of importance.

To obtain a good result, _____ is imperative.

chilled

5. The boiled, baked and chilled puddings are the most popular in commercial food operations.

The three most popular puddings in commercial food operations are: boiled, baked, _____.

cold

6. The steamed pudding is generally served during the cold season as it tends to be heavy and is usually served with a hot sauce. This pudding can be served very attractively if care is taken with the final preparation.

Steamed pudding is generally served during the _____ season.

heavy-soggy

7. The souffle is adaptable to a la carte service. It must be made just before service to secure lightness and fluffiness or it will become heavy and soggy. Thus one can see that souffles are not a good choice for the cafeteria.

If not made just before service, a souffle will become_____and_____.

hard sauce

8. There are three basic sauces from which a great many varieties may be made by the addition of various ingredients. These are: cream sauce, fruit sauce and hard sauce.

The three basic sauces are cream sauce, fruit sauce and_____.

bacterial

9. Custard creams, milk custards, cream fillings, etc. must always be carefully made and handled, but precautions are especially important during the summer months, as creams and custards are perfect media for bacterial contamination and growth.

Creams and custards are perfect media for_____contamination and growth.

mixing-boiling

10. Pastry cream is a cream filling that plays an important part in the making of many desserts. Smoothness and flavor are especially important and, therefore, great care should be taken during the mixing and boiling process.

To obtain smoothness and flavor, great care should be taken during the _____ and _____processes.

REVIEW

1. What are two requisites for making good puddings?

2. What are five basic puddings?

3. Which three are the most popular in commercial food operations?

4. Why are souffles a poor choice for a cafeteria?

5. What are the three basic sauces for puddings and ice creams?

6. How is hard sauce always served?

7. Why must custard creams, etc. be carefully made and handled, especially during the summer months?

8. Name five precautions to take in connection with cream goods.

9. In connection with the mixing process for pastry cream, why is it most important that sugar and eggs should never be allowed to stand without mixing?

ECLAIRS AND CREAM PUFFS

ECLAIR—A cream puff in an oblong shape is called an eclair. The name is French and literally translated means "lightning." Though cream puffs and eclairs are made from the same ingredients, eclairs are considered more festive and elegant than cream puffs; why, no one knows.

Eclairs are made with a chou (pronounced shoo) pastry, filled with cream fillings, whipped cream, or ice cream, and glazed with chocolate, vanilla, or coffee icing. They can be frozen, but most devotees prefer fresh eclairs.

Chou or cream-puff pastry is made by adding flour to boiling water and butter and cooking the mixture until a thick paste is formed. Then the eggs are beaten in, one at a time. The eggs make the paste, which is nothing but a thick sauce, puff up during cooking. When finished the puffs are cut open and filled with either a sweet or savory filling.

CREAM PUFF—This is an airy little cream-filled cake, brother to an eclair. Cream puffs are round, eclairs are oblong. They are of French origin and made by an entirely different method from other pastries. Cream-puff pastry is also called chou pastry or literally translated from the French "cabbage" pastry, because of the appearance of the finished product which bears a vague resemblance to a miniature cabbage.

Cooks should rid themselves of the idea that cream puffs are hard to make. As a matter of fact, they are one of the easiest pastries. They are also extremely useful since they make all sorts of delightful desserts or, if the filling is not sweet, elegant appetizers and garnishes.

a. chou   paste
b. the eggs con-
tained in the
paste.

1. Eclair paste (also called chou - shoo paste) is a paste which is between a batter and a dough consistency. It is made of bread flour, butter or shortening, eggs, water and salt.

The paste is used for making cream puffs and eclair shells, their small cousins the profiterolles, and French doughnuts (also called French crullers).

Popover batter is similar except that it is thinner in consistency than chou   paste and without fat. It must be well beaten to develop the gluten so that when steam explodes the batter, the new form will hold.

a.   Eclair paste is also known by its French name
_____.

b.   What do you suppose gives eclairs their yellow color? _____.

High to start.
(450°F. is used
for some items
to secure rapid
steam develop-
ment before the
product sets
and then when
full expansion
has occurred,
the temper-
ature is dropped
to complete
baking.)

2. The leavening agent in puff paste, choux paste and popover batter is steam. Steam develops in the areas where fat exists, between the sheets of dough in the puff paste and causes flaking. In the choux paste and popover, the steam formed inside pushes the paste of batter up or out making a large hollow inside. Continued baking causes the shell around the hollow to form from coagulation and gelatinization. Baking must continue until this wall is quite firm and will not collapse when the product is removed from the oven and the steam pressure subsides. Actually the shell is partially dried out in the baking to give it strength.

What do you think oven temperatures would be in products such as this that are leavened by steam? High or low?

The Nutritional Value of Baked Products

True

1. To find the nutritional value of a baked product, look at its ingredients. How much fat, how much protein and what kind of protein, how much sugar, how much starch, and how many vitamins are present?

Carbohydrates (starches and sugars) produce 4 calories per gram of energy for the body.

Fats, however, produce 9 calories per gram.

True or False: Fats produce 2-¼ times as much energy per gram as do carbohydrates or proteins.

True, although
a few contain
little fat and,
therefore, less
calories.

2. Calories are only one measure of nutritional value. An adult eats between about 2,000 and 6,000 calories a day, depending upon his size and energy output. The usual adult can do with less than 3,000 calories a day whereas the huge professional football player needs twice that amount. (U. S. Military Academy at West Point allows for 4,200 calories per day per man.)

Nearly all baked products contain large amounts of calories.

4-inch cut of apple pie—330 calories
1 doughnut—136 calories
1 sweet roll—178 calories
1 plain roll—120 calories
1 slice ½ inch white bread—63 calories
1 slice ½ inch whole wheat bread—55 calories

True or False: It is safe to say that most baked products are high in calories.

Both are
high in fat.

3. A graham cracker contains 27 calories while a 2-inch saltine cracker contains 12 calories. Why would such comparatively small pieces of food contain so many calories?

4. Calorie count is only one aspect of nutrition. Calories provide only energy. Living tissue, however, needs to replace itself and to grow. For this it needs protein. In addition to containing carbon, hydrogen or oxygen, protein also contains nitrogen.

Most baked goods are a good source of protein in that the flour used contains anywhere from about 6 to 15% protein.

For example, white bread is about 9% protein. Angel food cake, rich in eggs, contains about 7% protein. Most cakes run about 4 to 5% protein.

Compared with flesh foods (meat, fish, poultry), baked products have a little less than ½ as much protein present.

True or False: Most baked goods are fairly high in protein.

True for dough products. Dessert products, which contain much more fat and sugar, are not especially good sources of protein.

true

5. The quality of proteins varies considerably, depending upon how much of the essential amino acids the protein contains. The essential amino acids are needed by the human body each day for best nutrition.

Nearly all cereals, including wheat, are deficient in one of the amino acids, lysine. Wheat is also somewhat deficient in another of the essential amino acids, tryptophan.

Because of these deficiencies, protein from wheat does not have the same value to the body as do proteins from animals, such as meat, fish, poultry and dairy products.

True or False: Although flour contains a fair amount of protein, the protein is not of the same value to the body as are proteins from animals.

6. To overcome the lysine deficiency in flour, some bakers add ½ to 1% lysine to their flour. This greatly increases the protein value of the flour. Adding soy flour also increases the value of the wheat protein. The soy bean has more than enough lysine in it. The soy bean is a remarkable plant in that its beans contain 30-36% protein.

Wheat flour is deficient in what 2 essential amino acids?

build or
replace
body cells

7. Proteins are the raw materials for the growth of new body cells or their replacement. They are complex molecules containing nitrogen. Proteins, like all food materials, are made up of molecules. In proteins, molecules are grouped together to form amino acids.

When we eat bread the proteins in the gluten and the other proteins present break down into amino acids in the digestion process. These are then reassembled by the body to build or replace the body cells.

While starch and fat are used principally to provide energy for the body, protein is necessary to _____.

starch

8. Flour contains about 70% by weight of starch. In the diet it is the source of energy and, if not burned as energy, is converted into fat. During the baking process when the starch is heated in the presence of water some of the starch soaks up water and swells (gelatinizes). On drying it helps to form the bulk of the baked dough.

Along with gluten _____ helps to give a baked product its bulk and structure.

Yes; name one
that isn't.

9. Interestingly enough, starch can be broken down (hydrolyzed) into simple sugars. Both sugars and starches are of the same overall class of food materials called carbohydrates.

Carbohydrates are principally used by the body to provide energy or body fat. Are nearly all baked goods high in carbohydrates?

10. Another aspect of the nutritional value of a food is its vitamin content. Vitamins are substances that are essential in small amounts to regulate the metabolic processes of the body.

true

The whole wheat grain is high in the B vitamins (thiamine, niacin and riboflavin). The wheat germ containing fat is high in vitamin A.

True or False: The whole grain of wheat is a good source of vitamins A and the B complex of vitamins.

B

11. When flour is made from the whole wheat kernel most of the A and B vitamins are removed in the germ and the bran. The iron present is lost.

Since 1941, millers and bakers have "enriched" flour by adding back, and then some, the B vitamins and iron. Today the Federal Government, 30 states and Puerto Rico require that flour be "enriched". About 90% of all commercially baked standard white bread is "enriched".

Enriched flour has been "enriched" by adding back to the flour the ____ vitamins and iron.

D

12. Some flour is further enriched by the addition of calcium and vitamin ____.

thiamine, niacin and riboflavin

13. What are the B vitamins?

false, although this is widely believed.

14. True or False: Whole wheat bread is more nutritious than white bread.

puff pastry, doughnuts, or Danish pastry

15. Name two bakery products which contain more than 20% fat.

false, the body needs about 20-25% of its total calories in the form of fat.

16. According to the nutritionists, we should cut out eating all fat.

1.5 to 2 times more polyunsaturated fats should be eaten than saturated ones.

17. Which types of fat, saturated or unsaturated, should be eaten if we are concerned about the buildup of cholesterol in the blood system?

many have little or no fat; angel food cake and Italian bread are examples.

18. Many baked products are high in fat. Puff pastry is layers of fat and high gluten dough. Pastry shells are about 1/3 fat. Here are some other high fat baked products:

> Yeast raised doughnuts—27%
> Danish pastry—23%
> Assorted cookies—20% or higher
> Chocolate cake icing—14%
> Devil's Food cake—12%
> Apple pie—11%
> Coffee cake—10%

Where there is fat, there are calories, maybe more than is needed by the person eating the food. But, fat tastes so good and produces such a delectable texture in such items as cream puffs and Napoleons!

Would you guess that all baked goods are relatively high in fat?

Some are, some are not. It depends on the number of calories they contain.

19. Some fat is needed by the body. The problem is how much and what kind. Fat eaten by North Americans may run as much as 40% of the total calories taken in. Fat should constitute about 20-25% of the total calorie intake.

Much of the fat eaten is "hidden". It is part of foods not ordinarily thought of as high fat foods. Examples are hamburger, nuts, cheese, and avocados.

Can we say that all baked goods are fattening?

20. Depending on the number of double bond carbon linkages, fats are known as saturated, unsaturated or polyunsaturated. Saturated fats contain only single bond carbon linkages and are the least active chemically.

$$\begin{array}{ccc} H & & H \\ | & & | \\ -C & - & C- \\ | & & | \\ H & & H \end{array}$$

Mono unsaturated fats contain one double bond.

$$\begin{array}{ccc} H & & H \\ | & & | \\ -C & = & C- \end{array}$$

Some fats are naturally saturated which means that they have their full complement of hydrogen atoms. At room temperature such fats are likely to be plastic; oils are usually less saturated and are liquid at room temperature.

Whether or not a fat is saturated, unsaturated or polyunsaturated depends on the number of double bonds it contains. If no double bonds are present, the fat is known as _____ .

21. If only one double bond is present in a fat, it is known as a _____.

22. If more than one double bond is present in a fat, it is known as a _____.

23. Vegetable oils are likely to be polyunsaturated. Animal fats are likely to be saturated.

To make vegetable oil more plastic for use in baking, some hydrogen is added to the oil. Then it becomes more saturated.

Oils are likely to be polyunsaturated while hydrogenated fats and animal fats are more _____.

141

24. Too much polyunsaturated fat can be harmful. Nutritionists who are studying the problem of fat and the formation of cholesterol in the body say that we should take in about 1.5 to 2 times more polyunsaturated fats than saturated ones. Apparently, the unsaturated fats allow the cholesterol to pass through the intestinal walls and out of the body. If we eat only saturated fats and do not take enough exercise, cholesterol can build up in the blood system and deposit inside the blood vessels.

About 20-25% of the total calories we eat should be in the form of fat and we should have more/less polyunsaturated fats than the saturated types.

true; this practice is being recommended by many nutritionists.

25. True or False: When eating any animal fat such as is found in milk, cheese, egg yolks or meat, eat some polyunsaturated fat along with it such as found in special margarine, in special vegetable shortening, or in salad dressings.

saturated fat; butter is an animal fat.

26. Baked products that use only butter as the shortening contain a polyunsaturated/saturated fat.

not necessarily; the non-fat milk has had the butter fat removed and the vegetable shortening can be polyunsaturated.

27. True or False: Baked products containing non-fat dry milk and vegetable shortening are certain to contain saturated fats.

28. Does bread contain predominantly saturated or unsaturated fats?

Most bread would contain predominantly saturated fats unless made from a special vegetable shortening (most commercial breads are still made from lard!)

29. Many baked products contain sugar. Sugar does nothing for the body except provide energy. It contains no vitamins and does not replace or build tissues. Sugar that is not burned as energy in the body is converted into fat and stored. Is sugar good for us?

It depends on whether it is needed and how much you consume of it. Some nutritionists believe that sugar can be a cause of high blood pressure and heart disease.

30. Generally speaking, baked dough products are highly nutritious and are likely to contain vitamins A, the B complex and sometimes D. Dough products are a good source of the calcium needed for bone growth. They are a good source of protein although they are not as useful to the body as similar amounts of animal protein.

All baked goods are a good source of energy.

Are baked products fattening?

Any food is fattening if it contains large amounts of calories or if eaten excessively and in amounts in excess of what the body needs. No food is fattening if taken in a quantity that can be utilized by the body.

No; the yellow
pigments are re-
moved or
bleached out
and wheat germ
which contains
most of the
vitamin A has
been removed.

31. When we remove the bran and the germ from
the wheat kernel we remove most of the B vitamins, the iron and vitamin A.

The yellow pigments called the carotenoids
contain what is used to make vitamin A in the
body. Would you expect white flour to contain
vitamin A?

They should
avoid those
items which
are high in fat.
The rest of the
baked items are
no higher in
fat than other
foods and are
highly nutritious.

32. Many people on diets feel that baked products
are something they should avoid completely in
their diet. Is such a belief justifiable?

Some are, some
are not. Items
which require
much labor to
produce cost
more. Flour
itself, at about
10¢ a pound,
is one of the
cheapest foods
we can buy.

33. Are baked products economical from the
point of view of the nutritional value purchased?

REVIEW

1. Three broad classifications of food materials from the point of view of nutrition are fats, proteins and _____ .

2. Each gram of fat introduces _____ calories of energy.

3. Each gram of protein or carbohydrate produces _____ calories per gram.

4. True or False: All baked goods are fattening.

5. Is bread a good source of protein?

6. Which cake is the highest in protein?

7. Wheat would be an excellent source of well balanced protein except that it is deficient in two amino acids _____ and _____ .

8. What can be added to flour to be used in making bread to increase its effectiveness as a source of protein?

9. Of the principal food ingredients—protein, carbohydrates and fats—which is absolutely necessary for the replacement of tissue?

10. Would you say that bread is a good source of vitamin A?

11. Enriched flour has had what added to it?

12. True or False: "Enriched" bread is high in vitamins A and C.

13. When flour is milled the bran is removed. With the bran goes some of the vitamins. To replace these lost vitamins, flour is enriched by the addition of thiamine, niacin, iron and riboflavin. Thiamine, niacin and riboflavin are part of the B complex vitamins. Thiamine is also known as vitamin B_1. Riboflavin is also known as vitamin _____ .

14. "Enriched" flour has had the B vitamins and _____ added to it.

15. Vitamin B₁ is also known as _____ .

16. Since most of the vitamins have been removed in the milling process, would you think that white bread is less nutritious than whole wheat bread?

17. How about rye bread? Is it more nutritious than white bread?

FLOURS AND MEALS

I.   REASONS FOR IMPORTANCE OF FLOUR

II.   WHEAT
   1. Hard Wheat
   2. Soft Wheat
   3. The Milling of Wheat into Flour

III.   RYE FLOUR

IV.   RYE FLOUR, GRADES

V.   PUMPERNICKEL FLOUR

VI.   RYE BLEND FLOUR OR RYE FLOUR, BOHEMIAN

VII.   SELF-RISING FLOUR

VIII.   POTATO FLOUR

IX.   CORN FLOUR

X.   CORN MEAL

XI.   RICE FLOUR

XII.   ALL PURPOSE OR FAMILY FLOUR

XIII.   GLUTEN FLOUR

XIV.   GRAHAM FLOUR

XV.   BLEACHED FLOUR

XVI.   IDENTIFYING HARD AND SOFT FLOURS

XVII.   STRONG AND WEAK FLOURS

XVIII.   ENRICHED FLOUR

XIX.   BREAD FLOUR

Flours and Meals

Flour is the finely ground meal of wheat and is one of the most important ingredients used in bakery products. Therefore, flour quality has a major influence on the quality of the finished baked products.

I. REASONS FOR IMPORTANCE OF FLOUR

    A.   It is the backbone and structure of baked goods.
    B.   It acts as a binding agent and an absorbing agent.
    C.   It affects the keeping quality of products.
    D.   It is important to the flavor of products.
    E.   It adds nutritional value to the baked product.

II. WHEAT

Wheat, from which flour is made, is the most essential grain used in breadmaking because it is the only cereal that contains the proper combination of glutenin and gliadin. When combined with water, these properties form gluten, essential for retaining the gas produced by yeast. No other grain can replace wheat in bread making.

The primary types of wheat flour used in baking are hard wheat and soft wheat.

    1.   Hard Wheat
    There are several kinds of hard wheat:
        a. One hundred per cent straight flour is a strong type of flour. It is preferred in the production of quality hard rolls and hearth breads. Here it produces the best results.

        b. Patent Flour is generally used when a formula calls for bread flour. It is used in making bread, rolls, and the usual products made with bread flour.

        c. First clear flour and second clear flour are used in making rye breads because of their darker color and higher gluten content.

        d. Bran is used mainly in the production of muffins.

        e. Whole wheat flour (including graham) is used primarily in making whole wheat bread and muffins.

The Milling of Wheat into Flour

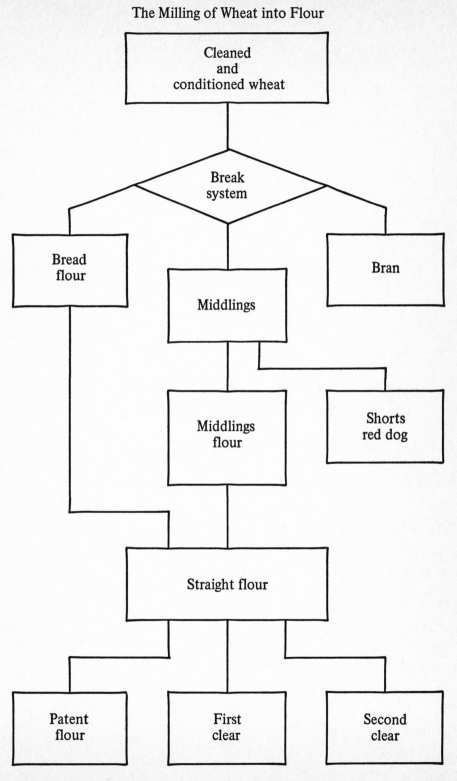

2. Soft Wheat

There are three kinds of soft wheat:
1. Cake flour is used to produce high-quality cakes.
2. & Pastry flour and cookie flour are used for pie crust,
3. cookies, and pastry.

The foregoing diagram shows the general separation of the various grades of flour, but does not show the exact system of the separation of flour streams.

This chart reprinted from a TREATISE ON CAKE MAKING by permission of Standard Brands, Inc., copyright owner.

III.   RYE FLOUR

Rye flour is secured from the milling of the rye berry or grain. While the composition of rye is quite similar to that of wheat, insofar as the actual amount of moisture, protein, carbohydrate, fat and ash are concerned, the nature or kind of protein in wheat and rye is quite different.

While some of the gluten components are present in rye, it is a well known fact that when rye flour is made into a dough by the addition of water, it does not form gluten such as is formed when wheat flour is treated in the same manner.

In making rye bread, some wheat flour is necessarily used as a source of gluten so that a porous well-risen loaf may result.

If rye flour were used alone, the loaf secured would naturally be heavy and somewhat soggy, with a consequent impairment of its palatability and digestibility.

Rye is milled into flours of different grades such as rye patent flour, rye straight flour, various dark rye flours, and Pumpernickel.

IV.   RYE FLOUR, GRADES

There are four grades of rye flour: (1) Light--practically as white in color as wheat flour, intended for use in rye products where a white color is desirable, but does not have the strong rye flavor of the darker grades; (2) Medium--darker in color because it contains a larger percentage of the rye grain, which also accounts for its pronounced rye flavor and, therefore, its popularity; (3) Dark--contains some of the outer part of the grain, used principally by bakers in making very dark rye bread; (4) Straight--consists of about 70 percent light flour and about 30 percent dark flour, often used interchangeably with the medium grade.

150

V. PUMPERNICKEL FLOUR

This is a coarsely ground, whole-rye flour. It is quite dark and is used chiefly in making pumpernickel bread. This flour is known in some sections as rye meal and rye graham, a 100% coarsely chopped rye, also known as rye meal.

VI. RYE BLEND FLOUR OR RYE FLOUR, BOHEMIAN

While rye contains some gluten, it is not sufficient to give satisfactory results in baking if rye flour alone is used. Rye flour is generally blended with a certain proportion of wheat flour in order to give it rising power.

RYE MEAL. (SEE PUMPERNICKEL FLOUR)

VII. SELF-RISING FLOUR

This is ordinary flour to which calcium acid phosphate, baking soda, and salt have been added. As calcium acid phosphate and baking soda are the ingredients of phosphate baking powder, self-rising flour is the same mixture obtained by the housewife when she mixes flour with baking powder and salt. However, the baking powder ingredients and the salt used in preparing the self-rising flour are mixed with the flour much more thoroughly and uniformly at the mill than they can possibly be mixed in the home; they cost the consumer less than if the baking powder and salt were bought separately; and the use of self-rising flour does away with the work of mixing the ingredients in the kitchen.

VIII. POTATO FLOUR

Used in the making of potato bread by mixing it with either wheat or rye flour. It is also used in making of bread.

ENTIRE WHEAT FLOUR OR WHOLE WHEAT (See Graham Flour.)

IX. CORN FLOUR

This flour is produced by pulverizing white corn grits.

X. CORN MEAL

This is the coarsely ground kernel of the corn, either yellow or white. The yellow corn meal is a very good source of vitamin A; white corn meal is lacking in this vitamin. The term "old process" is used in connection with corn meal; it is manufactured by grinding the entire kernel, with the exception of just the outer bran coat. In manufacturing the "new process" corn meal, the germ, which contains the corn oil, and all of the bran is removed. The "new process" corn meal keeps better because of the lack of oil, but the "old process" article, because of the oil in the germ, is decidedly superior, both in food value and in flavor.

XI.　　RICE FLOUR

Rice flour is produced by grinding uncoated rice. It is used like pastry flour and is also used in many diets where other flours are objectionable.

XII.　　ALL PURPOSE OR FAMILY FLOUR

This flour, also known as blend flour, as all-purpose and as general purpose flour, is a flour so prepared that it may be used quite satisfactorily for all baking and cooking purposes in the home. It may be a blend of hard wheat flours, a blend of soft wheat flours, or a blend of both hard and soft wheat flours. As a rule, family flour prepared from hard wheat flours is superior for making yeast breads, while that prepared from soft wheat flours is superior for making quick breads.

XIII.　　GLUTEN FLOUR

Gluten flour is made from hard wheat flour from which a large part of the starch has been removed. It is used for making bread for diabetics and others who must abstain from starchy foods.

XIV.　　GRAHAM FLOUR

There is no difference between graham flour, whole-wheat flour and entire-wheat flour. The terms are used interchangeably for the product made by grinding the entire wheat grain, including the bran—a 100 percent wheat flour.

XV.　　BLEACHED FLOUR

Flour requires proper aging in order to produce best results in baking. Storing newly milled flour for two or three months not only gives the flour the necessary aging, but also gives it a much whiter color—a whiteness consumers generally expect in flour of high quality. In order to eliminate the expense of storing the flour and in order to place the newly milled flour on the market immediately after it is milled, flour now commonly is bleached by chemicals, approved by food officials, which in no way affect the palatability or nutritive properties of the flour. The bleaching process also gives the new flour the proper aging, so that it is ready for use as it leaves the mill. All flour thus artificially bleached and aged is known as bleached flour.

XVI.   IDENTIFYING HARD AND SOFT WHEAT FLOURS

When hard wheat flour is rubbed between the fingers, it feels dry and somewhat granular. If a tablespoonful or so of the flour is pressed tightly in the hand, then shaken, it falls to powder readily, showing practically no imprint of the fingers. When soft wheat flour is rubbed between the fingers, it feels smooth and soft. If a tablespoonful or so of the flour is pressed tightly in the hand, then shaken, it remains more or less in lumps, showing the imprint of the fingers.

XVII.   "STRONG" AND "WEAK" FLOURS

Whether a flour is strong or weak depends upon the gluten that can be developed in it. When liquid is added to the flour, two of the flour proteins combine to form gluten, an elastic substance that gives the doughs and batters their ability to stretch. Good quality gluten is very elastic; it can easily "double in bulk" without breaking. Flour that contains this high quality gluten is called "strong" flour. It is made from hard wheat and is the baker's first choice for making yeast bread. A strong flour absorbs more liquids than a weak one and thus makes more loaves of bread than could be made from the same quantity of a weak flour. In weak flours, the gluten is less in quantity and weaker in quality than it is in strong flours—just right for making cakes and pastry. Weak flours are made from soft wheat.

XVIII.   ENRICHED FLOUR

This is a white flour, containing certain minimum amounts of at least two important vitamins and one added mineral. These added food values (vitamin B-1, nicotinic acid and iron) help to replace those lost from the wheat grain in the process of milling refined flour. Enriched flour may also contain certain amounts of two other vitamins; riboflavin and vitamin D, and two minerals, calcium and phosphorous, the adding of these, however, is optional.

The added vitamins and minerals do not change the flavor of the flour, nor do they change its color, appearance, and its baking and keeping qualities. The minimum requirements for added food values in enriched flour per pound are: 1.66 milligrams of vitamin B-1 (thiamine), 6.15 milligrams of nicotinic acid, 6.15 milligrams of iron. (Nicotinic acid is a vitamin found naturally in wheat and other foods. It is a pellagra-preventative factor—often referred to as the anti-pellagra vitamin—and has none of the qualities of nicotine found in tobacco.)

Creamy-colored enriched flour is made by a special milling process, which retains in the flour the amounts of vitamins and minerals that are lost in the ordinary method of milling refined wheat flour. Actually, such flour has not been enriched ; it is already rich—as it comes from the mill--in the vitamins and minerals required for "enriched" flours. While it is labeled "enriched", nothing has been added to it either during or after the milling process. It has its own nature-given vitamins and minerals, instead of having synthetic food values added to it.

Enriched Flour has synthetic vitamins added, which serve the same purpose in the diet as the natural vitamins.

XIX.   BREAD FLOUR

This is a hard wheat flour, usually a blend of hard winter and hard spring wheat flours, sold both bleached and unbleached, and used largely by the bakery trade for making bread. It is slightly granular to the touch and yields gluten that is quite strong and elastic.

Flour should be stored in a cool, dry place. A temperature of 65° to 70°F. will be satisfactory. The storage room should be well ventilated and free from any odors whatsoever. Flour readily absorbs odors that often prove ruinous to the finished baked product.

RYE BREAD AND RYE FLOUR

I.   POINTS OF INTEREST CONCERNING THE PRODUCTION OF RYE BREAD

A.   There are many different kinds of rye bread made and sold in this country, ranging from dark, sour rye to a very light rye loaf.

B.   The flavor of rye bread depends on process of fermentation employed and on the quantity and quality of the flour used for the blend.

c.   Rye flour is more apt to ferment than white wheat flour, The fermentation period of rye doughs, especially those in which sour is used, must be carefully watched and regulated.

D.   Care should be taken to avoid the use of excessive steam in the oven during the baking of rye bread.

II.   RYE FLOUR - RYE BLEND FLOUR - PUMPERNICKEL MEAL OR FLOUR

A.   Rye flour is flour secured from the milling of the rye berry or grain.
    (1)   When rye flour is made into dough by the addition of water, it does not form gluten as wheat flour does. Therefore, some wheat flour is used as a source of gluten so that a porous, well-risen loaf may result.

154

(2) Rye is milled into flours of different grades such as rye patent flour, rye straight flour and various dark rye flours.

B. Rye Blend Flour is usually made by mixing from 25% to 40% of Rye Flour with Baker's Clear. The exact amount of Rye Flour used depends on local conditions and the character of the bread desired.

C. Pumpernickel Flour is a coarsely ground, whole-rye flour. It is quite dark and is used chiefly in making pumpernickel bread.

III. TYPES OF RYE BREAD

A. Most popular types of rye bread are made with either a straight or sponge dough, sometimes plain or with caraway seeds.

(1) Plain rye bread
(2) Light rye bread
(3) Dark rye bread
(4) Bohemian rye
(5) Jewish rye
(6) Swedish rye
(7) Pumpernickel rye

B. These breads may be made with or without sour.

IV. PREPARATION OF SOUR

4 lbs. of sour* taken from Jewish shop
   To this add:
2 qts. of water
5 lbs. of dark rye flour   1st sour
   Let stand 3 hours and add
4 qts. of water
10 lbs. of dark rye flour   2nd sour
   Let stand 3 hours and add
12 qts. of water
30 lbs. of dark rye flour   3rd and final sour

*If it is impossible to secure this sour as a starter, it may be started as follows:

Mix together: 2 lbs. rye flour
                       1½ lbs. water
                       1 large onion (split into 4 parts)
                       6 oz. ground caraway seed
                       2 oz. Fleischmann's Yeast
Let stand 24 hours.

When sour starter is used, remove the onion and proceed as described above.

These sours should be made 3 hours apart. See that these sours are not made too stiff. Temperature of water for these sours should be 60°F. in summer and 80°F. in winter.

If more than one batch is required, arrange to take 30 lbs. from 3rd and final sour, adding 12 qts. of water and 30 lbs. of dark rye flour, which makes again 84 lbs. of sour. In this manner, continuous batches can be made as required.

Always leave enough sour for use the following day as shown above. Use ½ lb. of sour for every 10 lbs. of final sour required.

REVIEW

1. What is flour?

2. What are some reasons for the importance of flour?

3. Why is wheat the most essential grain used in bread-making?

4. What are the two primary types of wheat flour used in baking?

5. Why is rye flour alone not recommended for making bread?

6. What is all-purpose or family flour?

7. Why is flour bleached?

8. What is "strong" flour, what is it made from, and what is it used for?

9. What is "weak" flour, what is it made from, and what is it used for?

10. What is enriched flour?

11. How should flour be stored?

Sugars and Syrups

I.   GENERAL INFORMATION

II. PURPOSES SERVED BY SUGARS

III. CLASSIFICATION OF SUGARY AGENTS
   A.   Disaccharides
      1. Cane and Beet Sugar
      2. Brown Sugar
      3. Malt Sugar
      4. Lactose or Milk Sugar

   B.   Monosaccharides
      1. Corn Syrup (Dextrose)
      2. Levulose

   C.   Sugar Syrups and Moisture Retaining Agents.
      1. Molasses
      2. Malt Syrup
      3. Invert Sugar (Standardized)
         a.   Definition
         b.   Commercial Preparation
         c.   Functions in Cake Making
         d.   Amount and Manner of Use
      4. Honey
      5. Glucose Syrup (Corn Syrup)

IV. STORAGE

I. GENERAL INFORMATION

Webster's <u>New International Dictionary,</u> Second Edition, una-bridged, gives this definition: "SUGAR: A sweet crystallizable sub-stance, colorless or white when pure, occurring in many plant juices and forming an important article of food . . . . The chief sources of sugar are the sugar cane and the sugar beet, the completely refined products of which are identical."

By definition, therefore, and by long-established common usage, sugar means sucrose (beet or cane sugar) and nothing else. The word "sugars", however, can refer in the chemical sense to the family of car-bohydrates known as the saccharides, any member of which is correctly called a "sugar" – but not simply "sugar". Chemists recognize dozens of sugars of varying sweetness such as <u>milk</u> sugar (lactose), <u>corn</u> sugar, (dextrose) and <u>malt</u> sugar (maltose). Maple sugar is largely sucrose, but is distinguished by its flavor.

REFINED SUGAR
The refined, granulated sugar of commerce is derived from sugar cane and sugar beets. It is 99.94 per cent pure, and is thus the purest of all organic substances produced in anything near comparable volume. Sugar is distinguished by (a) its lack of flavor other than sweetness, (b) its ability to blend other flavors and accentuate aromas, (c) its ready solubility in water, and (d) its high caloric value. It is pleasant to the taste, clean, uniform in quality, easily assimilated, contains no waste and keeps indefinitely.

II. PURPOSES SERVED BY SUGARS

Sugar as a whole serves the following important purposes in baking:
1. Adds sweetness.
2. Aids in the creaming process.
3. Creates a softening or spreading action of batter.
4. Imparts crust color.
5. Retains moisture in loaf, prolonging freshness. *main function.*
6. Forms body of icings and fillings.
7. Adds food value.
8. Aids in the fermentation of yeast.

III. CLASSIFICATION OF SUGARY AGENTS

The principal groups of sugars used in baking are "Disaccharides" and "Monosaccharides". Each contains several different types of sugars commonly used in the bakery. In addition to these two groups of sugars, we have a third group of sugary agents that include sugary syrups.

A. DISACCHARIDES
1. Cane and Beet Sugar
Without further qualification, the single word "sugar", as ordinarily employed and as used in this book, refers to that form of sugar secured principally from the sugar cane and beet. This sugar is known technically as "Sucrose". Frequently, refined sucrose, regardless of its source, is spoken of as "cane" sugar or "common" sugar. As purchased today in its white form, this sugar is nearly 100% pure.

Sugar of the same high purity may be obtained in different degrees of fineness or size of granule. This difference has a marked effect on the value of the sugar when used for various purposes in cake making.

TYPES & USES

Granulated Sugar
Ultra-fine: Especially suited for cake work in the bakery and in dry mixes, such as dessert powders, and cake mixes and for coating confectionery pan goods.

Very fine: Ideal for dry mixing with other finely divided materials in the production of cake mixes, pudding preparations, gelatine dessert powders and the like.

Fine or Extra fine: This is "regular" granulated sugar used for all-purpose, general food and beverage manufacture. It is the type of sugar usually served at the table.

Medium coarse: Generally employed in the production of crystallizing syrups in confectionery and in fondant-making, where an unusually white product is required. It is well adapted to the manufacture of cordials. Medium coarse is a "strong" sugar which resists color changes and inversion in high temperature cooking.

Coarse: Sometimes preferred for the purposes to which a medium-coarse grain sugar is put.

Special sugars: These have been carefully tested to meet the critical requirements of commercial canners and soft drink manufacturers.

Powdered Sugars

Ultra-fine (Confectioners' 10X type): Recommended for smoothest-textured frostings and icings, and uncooked fondants.

Very fine (Confectioners' 6X type): Recommended for cream fillings in biscuit work, and for sprinkling on buns, pies and pastries. It is also suitable for uncooked fondants, frostings and icings. It mixes well with melted fats to make certain confectioners' coatings.

Fine (Confectioners' 4X type): Used in the manufacture of lozenges and chewing gum, and in packing such confections as marshmallows and Turkish paste. Extensively employed in chocolate manufacture, it is also used for a finish coating for pan goods where a smooth surface is needed.

Medium coarse: Generally applicable to dusting mixtures where other powdered sugars are too fine, and the product is prone to accumulate surface moisture. It is used for dusting doughnuts and crullers.

Confectioners' sugars are usually packed with small amounts of corn starch to prevent caking.

2. Brown Sugar

Brown sugar is cane or beet sugar in which the refining process has not been completed. It is sometimes spoken of as soft sugar because of its characteristic soft feel. Such sugar naturally has a tendency to "cake" in storage. Various grades of brown sugar are produced containing from about 85% to 92% of sucrose together with a small amount of invert sugar. Turbinado sugars, although not so white as highly refined granulated sugars, also are enonomically advantageous in a wide variety of products.

The characteristic flavor and color of brown sugar are due to the caramel and other substances present in the natural sugar syrup before refining. The lower grades of brown sugar possess a more pronounced molasses like taste than the higher grades. Brown sugar can be used advantageously in certain dark cake mixes and icings, especially where its characteristic flavor is desired.

3. Malt Sugar

Malt sugar or maltose, as the name implies, is the chief constituent of malt syrup, and when malt syrup is used in bakery products, some malt sugar is thereby introduced into the dough. The use of malt syrup in cakes will be explained later under "Syrups".

4. Lactose, or Milk Sugar

Lactose is the natural sugar of milk. It is often termed milk sugar. While obtainable, it is not used as such in bakery products but is carried into the batter by the milk used. While of relatively low sweetening value, lactose is a good food value, and contributes to crust color.

B. MONOSACCHARIDES

Sugars coming under this classification are often termed "simple" sugars. While the different sugars in this group have the same chemical composition, they vary considerably in their degree of sweetness and other physical characteristics. The principal "monosaccharides" of interest are:

1. Corn Sugar (Dextrose)

Dextrose is a form of sugar found in the bakery in the form of corn syrup. Dextrose is not as sweet as cane sugar. The corn sugar of commerce is manufactured from cornstarch. Various grades of corn sugar can be produced having a dextrose content of from about 80% to over 99% on a dry basis. In cake making, corn sugar is sometimes used in combination with cane or beet sugar and is often employed where excessive sweetness is not required.

2. Levulose

Levulose is a form of sugar often known as fruit sugar or fructose. It is of the same chemical composition as dextrose but is much sweeter, even sweeter than cane sugar. While levulose as such has not been commercially available to the baker, considerable research work is being done on it and it is quite possible that before many years it will become available in a pure form for bakers' use. Levulose is present in molasses. It is the principal sugar in honey and contributes 50% of Invert Sugar.

C. SUGARY SYRUPS AND MOISTURE RETAINING AGENTS

1. Molasses —sugar cane or beet.

The best grade of molasses used by the baker is a viscous sugary liquor obtained by concentrating the juice of sugar cane which has been previously treated in order to contain sufficient invert sugar to prevent crystallization. The brown color and characteristic flavor of molasses are due to the caramel and other substances derived from the original cane juice in the process of abstracting the sugar.

There are various grades or types of molasses, varying in composition and depending on the degree of refinement. In general, molasses contains approximately 35% to 50% sucrose, about 15% to 30% invert sugar, about 20% to 25% water, and from 2% to 5% mineral matter, together with a small amount of protein and other constituents.

Low grades of molasses are usually lower in sucrose content, higher in invert sugar content and mineral matter, and harsher in flavor than the higher grades of molasses. The invert sugar contained in molasses assists in prolonging freshness in cakes.

Molasses is used mainly in certain dark cakes and cookies where its peculiar flavor is considered desirable. In selecting molasses for use in cake making, its flavor should be of foremost consideration.

2. Malt Syrup

Malt syrup is a specially prepared concentrated syrup made by evaporating a water extract of malt under carefully controlled conditions. It is used primarily in yeast made products.

3. Invert Sugar (Standardized) _Lewich_

a. Definition *1:1 dextrose levulose*

Invert sugar is equal parts of the two simple sugars, "dextrose" and "levulose". Although sweeter than cane sugar, invert sugar is otherwise neutral in flavor. It is used commercially in cake and candy making, often in the form of a syrup which contains about 50% invert sugar, 30% sucrose and 20% water. It is also obtainable in either plastic or paste form. Invert sugar occurs naturally in honey and molasses. In bread doughs, invert sugar is formed from the cane or beet sugar present by the action of an enzyme known as invertase which is present in the yeast.

b. Commercial Preparation

Invert sugar is produced in the form of a syrup by heating a solution of cane or beet sugar to which has been added a small amount of acid, such as tartaric acid, or of invertase, an enzyme contained in yeast. Under these conditions the acid or invertase acts on the cane or beet sugar and converts it into the new form of sugar known as "invert".

While invert sugar may be a new idea to many bakers, it has been used for a number of years in candy and biscuit plants. Some bakers have been in the habit of making their own invert syrup, as described above, through the use of acids. However, in the average bakery, it is quite difficult to prepare a uniform invert sugar. The acid which is carried along in the invert syrup as it is made must be neutralized either prior to its incorporation in the cake mix or afterwards by the addition of the proper amount of soda. It is exceedingly difficult for the average baker to know just the correct amount of soda required and quite often this means either an excess of soda or an excess of residual acid remaining in the dough. Furthermore, in preparing invert sugar in a bakery by the use of acid there is some danger that the acid used may attack the metal of the container with decidedly detrimental results. Either of these conditions is undesirable and may be eliminated by the use of an invert sugar that has been commercially prepared under carefully controlled conditions and in which the acidity has been properly and correctly neutralized.

c.   Functions in Cake Making
i.   Prolongs Freshness
Invert sugar has the remarkable ability to hold or retain moisture. Thus the use of invert syrup aids in delaying the staling of the cake. It is especially valuable in sweet mixtures that have a tendency to dry out too rapidly.

ii.   Promotes Smoothness in Icings
The presence of some invert sugar prevents the crystallization or graining of cane or beet sugar. In this way, invert syrup promotes that smoothness desirable in many icings.

iii.   Sweetness
Invert syrup is very sweet and naturally imparts this characteristic to the finished cake.

iiii.   Crust Color
Invert sugar aids in the promotion of a rich, brown crust color.

d.   Amount and Manner of Use
In cakes of the pound cake class which are very slowly baked, the amount of invert sugar to be used without incurring a slight discoloration of the crumb is quite limited. In cakes which are baked faster, larger amounts may be employed with no such discoloration. For light fruit cake, use from 10% to 20%, and as high as 30% may be used for dark fruit cake. The amount employed in cup cake and plain layer cakes will range from 5% to 20%. In sponge cake, from 4% to 6% of the sugar may be replaced with invert sugar. The use of too much invert syrup, especially in light cakes, may affect the volume, cell structure and crumb color adversely.

The invert syrup may be creamed together with the remainder of the sugars used and the shortening, or it may be added to the creamed sugar-shortening mass at the completion of the creaming process. It may also be mixed with the milk or milk solution.

4.   Honey
One of the first sugary agents known to man is a natural invert syrup produced from the nectar of flowers through the agency of the honey-bee.

164

Honey varies in composition, depending on its source, but an average sample would contain about 75% invert sugar, about 15% to 20% water, and a small amount of other substances, some of which give honey its natural delicious flavor. This characteristic honey flavor which is not present in commercial invert syrup, is the principal reason for the use of honey in special types of cakes and cookies.

5. Glucose Syrup (Corn Syrup)

Glucose syrup, perhaps better known as "commercial glucose" or "corn syrup" is produced commercially from cornstarch. It varies somewhat in composition, depending on the manner of manufacture, but an average glucose syrup contains about 40% corn sugar, or dextrose, and a considerable amount of dextrin. It possesses some moisture retaining properties, probably because of its relatively high content of dextrin, and is used to some extent in both cakes and icings. It aids in the promotion of a glossy surface in certain types of icings.

IV. STORAGE

Storage of sugar should be in a cool dry place.

SUGAR COOKING

To cook sugar, approximately three parts sugar to one part water are placed in a copper or stainless steel pot and stirred until the mass comes to a boil. The sides of the pot are brushed with water to clear them of any sugar crystals. The formation of crystals will start a chain reaction of crystallization that makes the mixture grainy.

Another way of clearing the sides of the pot is to cover the pot while it boils, letting the steam from the syrup wash down the sides of the pot. This is a very important step in the early stages. Continue to cook the syrup until it reaches the proper proportion of water to sugar.

Expert confectioners usually judge the degree of the syrup by dipping the index finger into cold water and then immediately dipping the same finger into the boiling syrup. This method is definitely not recommended for a novice because of the danger involved. A candy thermometer should be used. While the thermometer is not in actual use, place it in a jar of warm water close to where the cooking takes place. This will eliminate the breakup which will occur if a cold thermometer were placed in hot syrup.

Boiling Stages

The chart below indicates the temperature reading for each stage of sugar that reflects the amount of water in the sugar. The less water present, the higher the temperature of the boiling sugar. The less water the more solid or harder is the sugar mixture when cooled. Temperatures may vary because of the difference in humidity and altitude conditions. Since it only takes a few degrees to bring syrup to another stage, temperature control is extremely important.

Stages of Sugar Boiling

Stages	Temperature Range
Thread	230°F.–235°F.
Soft Ball	240°F.–245°F.
Ball	250°F.–255°F.
Hard Ball	260°F.–265°F.
Small Crack	270°F.–275°F.
Crack	275°F.–280°F.
Hard Crack	285°F.–315°F.
Caramel	325°F.–350°F.

The chart below shows how the concentration of sugar is reflected in the temperature of boiling. As the concentration of sugar increases so too does the temperature at which the mixture boils. Knowing the boiling temperature also tells the concentration of sugar.

Boiling Points of Various Concentrations of Sugar and Water

Boiling Degree Water & Sugar	% of Sugar Present	% of Water Present
212.7°F.	10%	90%
213.8°F.	30%	70%
215.6°F.	50%	50%
223.7°F.	70%	30%
225.2°F.	75%	25%
238.8°F.	85%	15%
243.8°F.	87%	13%
249.5°F.	89%	11%
252.7°F.	90%	10%

REVIEW

1. What are the two chief sources of sugar?

2. Which of the following statements may be applied to the use of sugar?

   a. Aids in the creaming process.
   b. Imparts crust color.
   c. Retains moisture, thereby prolonging freshness.
   d. Aids in the fermentation of yeast.

3. What are the two main groups of sugars entering into bakery products?

4. What is brown sugar?

5. What is lactose?

6. Give two examples of "monosaccharides".

7. What is invert sugar composed of?

8. In what form is invert sugar generally used commercially?

9. How does the use of invert sugar delay the staling of cake?

10. How does the presence of invert sugar promote smoothness in icings?

11. Name a natural invert sugar.

12. From what is glucose syrup produced commercially?

Eggs and Egg Products

I.   GENERAL INFORMATION

II.   FUNCTION OF EGGS IN CAKE MAKING

     A.   Binding or Texturizing Action
     B.   Leavening Action
     C.   Shortening Action
     D.   Flavor or Eating Quality
     E.   Color
     F.   Food Value

III.   IMPORTANT CHARACTERISTICS OF EGGS

     A.   Body of Whites
     B.   Richness and Color of Yolks
     C.   Uniformity as to Wholesomeness
     D.   Uniformity as to other Properties
     E.   Size and Yield
     F.   Inferior Grades

IV.   CLASSIFICATION OF EGGS

     A.   Shell Eggs
     B.   Dried Eggs
     C.   Frozen Eggs

V.   TYPES OF FROZEN EGGS AND FROZEN EGG PRODUCTS

     A.   Frozen Whole Egg
     B.   Frozen Egg White
     C.   Frozen Egg Yolk
     D.   Fortified Eggs

VI.   ADVANTAGES OF HIGH QUALITY, SPRING-LAID FROZEN EGGS

     A.   Strictly Fresh Eggs Assured
     B.   Quality Frozen, Spring-Laid Eggs Reflected in Quality of Cake
     C.   Uniformity Insured
     D.   Time Saved in the Bakery
     E.   Economy Through the Elimination of Waste
     F.   Frozen Eggs Mean Greater Profits to the Baker

VII.   HANDLING FROZEN EGGS IN THE BAKERY

I. GENERAL INFORMATION

Eggs and egg products constitute important ingredients used by bakers principally in the production of cakes and sweet goods. In these products eggs and egg products comprise approximately one-half of the cost of the ingredients. In some cakes, such as sponge cake, the cost of eggs may amount to as much as 70 per cent of the total ingredient cost.

Eggs are commercially available to the baker in four forms: (1) shell eggs, (2) liquid eggs, (3) frozen eggs and (4) dried eggs. The separated whites and yolks may also be procured in liquid, frozen or dried form. Certain modified egg products, such as sugar yolks and glycerin yolks, are also produced for use by the baking industry. Because of cost and good quality frozen eggs are much more widely used in the bakery than fresh eggs. Dried eggs, despite advantages of exceptional keeping quality and convenient form, have failed to attain popularity with commercial bakers due chiefly to the adverse changes that occur in the egg material upon drying. Dried eggs are an important ingredient in most prepared cake mixes, however.

II. FUNCTION OF EGGS IN CAKE MAKING

Eggs are most widely used in cakes. Generally speaking, without eggs there would be no cake. They are the major factor in giving cake the dominant characteristics that differentiate cake from other baked products. The most important of these characteristics are:

A. Binding or Texturizing Action
The most essential factor in the making of a cake is the formation or development, in the mixing and the maintaining or retention in the baking, of cell structure. Eggs, (wholes, whites or yolks) hold together as an emulsion the other ingredients of a cake batter, the flour, the fat, the sugar and the moisture. Eggs are also of prime importance in the production of the smooth flowing batter that is necessary for proper handling of cake mixes in scaling or depositing machines.

B. Leavening Action
Beaten eggs form a fluffy, foam-like mass which is much lighter and occupies a much larger volume than the unbeaten egg. When this foam-like mass is added to other cake ingredients to make a cake batter, the foam structure makes up to a certain extent the cell structure of the cake. When the individual cells are subjected to the heat of the oven, the expansion of air, together with the vaporization of moisture in these bubbles or cells, tends to expand the cells and raise or leaven the cake.

This same final action or leavening in a cake can be obtained from eggs that are simply creamed into a sugar-shortening creamed mass. Here, the eggs tend to stabilize the air cells developed by creaming by rendering the cells elastic so that they can expand on heating without rupturing. This expansion raises the cake. Here, as before, the leavening is due to the expansion of air and the vaporization of moisture into the cells from the cell walls.

C.   Shortening Action

Approximately one-third of the egg yolk is fat which adds shortening value.

D.   Flavor or Eating Quality

Eggs have a characteristic flavor that cannot be duplicated. Fresh eggs impart a delicious flavor to a cake. Also, due to their texturizing effect, the eating quality of the cake is definitely enhanced.

E.   Color

Where whole egg, yolk or egg product containing egg yolk is used in cake mixes, color is of primary importance. Eggs produce in the cake that golden color which the housewife associates with richness of cake quality.

F.   Food Value

The nutritive value of eggs needs little explanation. Rich in fat, protein and essential mineral substances necessary to growth and health, eggs are rightly considered as one of mankind's basic foods. Naturally, their food value is imparted to the products in which they are used.

III.   IMPORTANT CHARACTERISTICS OF EGGS

In purchasing eggs for the purpose of cake making, the following points should be kept in mind.

A.   Body of Whites

A strong, firm-bodied white is desirable for cake baking, inasmuch as it whips up better and gives strength to the framework of the cake. A thin, watery white will produce soft, soggy cake devoid of lightness and fluffiness. Spring-laid eggs have the best type of whites. During and for some months after the molting season, which begins in July, the whites are usually weak. Spring-laid eggs are available throughout the entire year in the form of frozen eggs. In other words, eggs that are laid in the spring are promptly collected, candled, broken, inspected and frozen.

B. Richness and Color of Yolks

Spring-laid eggs excel on both these points—the yolks contain a higher percentage of fat and the color is much better than in eggs laid during the summer, fall and winter months. During the spring, hens have more opportunity to get fresh green fodder, which produces the preferred type of yolk. Egg yolk contributes richness, flavor, appetizing color, softness and nutritive value to a cake.

C. Uniformity as to Wholesomeness

A good baker sometimes runs into a lack of uniformity and wholesomeness, particularly in shell eggs. He finds musty eggs, "hay" eggs, and other types of inferior eggs. If shell eggs are bought, it is the better part of wisdom to buy them from a reliable house and pay a fair price to secure a high grade. A saving of 2 cents in the price of a dozen eggs is not always sound economy, for one bad egg out of a dozen may give a bad flavor to a batch of cake costing perhaps $2.00 or $3.00.

D. Uniformity as to Other Properties

It is essential that the eggs be uniform in other properties, such as the body of the whites and the color of the yolks. Shell eggs are likely to vary in quality from month to month.

E. Size and Yield

When buying shell eggs, buy according to yield. It may be found that a case of shell eggs, selling at 2 or 3 cents a dozen more than another grade, will actually produce more egg meat at a lower cost per pound than the cheaper eggs. This is because eggs vary so widely in size. Occasionally, exceedingly large eggs may be secured that will give a yield of 37 and 38 pounds of egg meat but, in other instances, with small eggs, the yield will not be over 28 or 30 pounds per case.

F. Inferior Grades

Deterioration in eggs is caused chiefly by bacterial action. "Cracks" may be a snare and delusion, because in the use of "cracks" there is a tremendous loss from leakage, that may far more than offset the difference in the price per dozen.

IV. CLASSIFICATION OF EGGS

Eggs, from the standpoint of the baker, may be classified as Shell Eggs, Dried Eggs and Frozen Eggs.

A. Shell Eggs

Shell eggs are ordinary hens' eggs as they are usually marketed to the baker in crates or cases of thirty dozen each. The quality of such Shell Eggs is determined by "candling" or "lighting" the egg.

This is done by holding the egg before a lighted opening, usually in a dark room, in such a manner that light rays pass through the shell and illumine the interior of the egg.

Various localities or cities may designate the same grade of Shell Eggs by different names, letters or numerals, and it is, accordingly, practically impossible to list classifications which would be applicable in all cases.

B.   Dried Eggs

At one time Dried Eggs were used to a considerable extent in certain types of bakery products. Today, however, Dried Eggs constitute only a small fraction of the total amount of eggs used in baking in the United States and Canada.

Dried Eggs are produced by removing the bulk of the moisture from liquid eggs. This is done by either a spray drying or a tray or pan drying process. Dried Eggs are usually available as Dried Whole Egg, Dried White (albumen), and Dried Yolk.

CONVERSION TABLE FOR DRIED EGGS

Type	Liquid Wt. Desired	Solids Needed	Water Required
Egg Whites	1 lb.	2 oz.	14 oz.
Whole Eggs	1 lb.	4¾ oz.	11¼ oz.
Fortified Eggs	1 lb.	5½ oz.	10½ oz.
Sugar Yolk	1 lb.	8 oz.	8 oz.

C.   Frozen Eggs

Frozen eggs are produced from shell eggs by removing the edible liquid and freezing it. After the packing and freezing process, the eggs are held in freezer storage at zero degrees Fahrenheit or below until withdrawn for delivery.

Definite standards for purchasing Frozen Eggs have not been adopted, due to the difficulty which would be experienced in grading the product either in its frozen state or by sampling. While shell eggs may be individually candled or "lighted" to determine their quality, the baker buying Frozen Eggs must depend principally on the reputation of the packer. It has, therefore, become advisable for the baker who desires top quality Frozen Eggs to purchase his requirements from a firm not only in a position to guarantee the quality of its products but experienced also in the handling and delivery to bakers of refrigerated products.

It is the combination of these two factors that has brought about the continued and steady increase in Frozen Egg consumption since 1928. This increased consumption has been accompanied by improvements in frozen egg processing and delivery.

The best quality Frozen Eggs present to the baker the most economical means of securing eggs for year-round use. They make it possible for him to have spring-laid eggs every season of the year.

V. TYPES OF FROZEN EGGS AND FROZEN EGG PRODUCTS

Frozen eggs are generally available in convenient ten and thirty pound cans in any of the following types:

A. Frozen Whole Egg

Frozen Whole Egg is the product as separated from the shell, packed and frozen. The suggested Government "Solids" specification is minimum 24% and maximum 28%. *egg white* → *whip to max volume : not enough*

B. Frozen Egg White

Frozen Egg White is that part of the edible egg which encloses and protects the egg yolk in the shell. It is almost pure albumen and, according to suggested Government Standards, should run from 11% to 13% Egg White Solids.

C. Frozen Egg Yolk

Frozen Egg Yolk is the separated yolk of the egg, which, in commercial separation, carries with it a small amount of egg white. Government specifications suggest minimum solids of 42.5% and maximum solids of 45%. *small amount of sugar to add moisture.*

D. Fortified Eggs

Whole Eggs to which extra yolks are added to give greater egg solids content than whole eggs.

VI. ADVANTAGES OF HIGH QUALITY, SPRING-LAID FROZEN EGGS

A. Strictly Fresh Eggs Assured

High quality, frozen, spring-laid eggs come from certain sections of the grain belt which produce the finest eggs in the country. These eggs are selected for their adaptability to the production of quality cake and sweet goods. This means that strictly fresh eggs are collected, brought to the plants and inspected, broken and inspected again and then frozen. In their frozen state, all their fine qualities are conserved intact.

B. Quality, Frozen, Spring-Laid Eggs Reflected in Quality of Cake

For high quality cake and sweet goods, the baker needs high quality eggs. It is mistaken economy to use inferior eggs which will offset the advantages of other costly cake ingredients. High quality, frozen, spring-laid eggs possess whites that are firm and have excellent whipping qualities, and yolks that are uniform and that enhance the eating qualities and golden color of the cake.

C.   Uniformity Insured

When high quality, frozen, spring-laid eggs are used, the baker is assured of uniformity in the various important functions performed by eggs in cake making. The use of shell eggs purchased throughout different seasons of the year represents a gamble insofar as uniformity is concerned. This is due to the fact that eggs vary in composition with the changing seasons and character of feed. The use of high quality, frozen, spring-laid eggs eliminates all worry on this score.

D.   Time Saved in the Bakery

The edible portion of the egg is made up of about 36% egg yolk and 64% egg white and it is on this basis that the baker purchasing shell eggs must accept them. He must break and remove the shells in order to obtain the whole egg. And if either egg white or egg yolk is desired separately, he must separate the white from the yolk which frequently results in an over-supply of one type.

The resultant labor cost, time lost, unsanitary procedure and over-supply of white or yolk have been eliminated by the use of frozen eggs. These may be purchased as needed, when needed and in accordance with the baker's requirements.

E.   Economy Through the Elimination of Waste

When shell eggs are employed, there is likely to be a loss through shrinkage, spoilage, and breakage, as well as in the process of breaking and separating the eggs at the bench. Furthermore, there is danger of one bad egg occasionally slipping in and spoiling a measure full. When high quality, frozen eggs are used the baker is insured against such a mishap.

F.   Frozen Eggs Mean Greater Profits to the Baker

When a crate of shell eggs is purchased by the baker, the proportion of yolks and whites is predetermined. In ordinary bake shop separation of shell eggs, the yield is about 19 pounds of whites and 16 pounds of yolks. When high quality, frozen eggs are employed, they can be purchased or withdrawn from the warehouse in the amounts and kinds to meet production needs. Day in and day out, this means an economy which should not be overlooked.

VII.   HANDLING FROZEN EGGS IN THE BAKERY

Frozen eggs, when they are delivered to the baker, are in a solid, frozen mass at a temperature of about 15 degrees above zero. Before they can be used they must be thawed out and mixed so as to secure uniform consistency. There are two ways in which frozen eggs

174

may be thawed prior to using, namely, to set out the eggs required for the day's baking in a temperate part of the shop, where they may thaw slowly, or to set them in running cool water.

The latter method is decidedly preferable. Frozen eggs will thaw out much more rapidly when the container of eggs is placed in running water than they will when merely exposed to air of the same or even somewhat higher temperature than that of running water.

At room temperature a can of frozen eggs may require from 18 to 24 hours for proper thawing, whereas it probably would be completely defrosted in from 5 to 6 hours if placed in a tank of cool, running water.

In bakeries where large quantities of frozen eggs are regularly used, the installation of a defrosting or thawing tank is a wise investment. There are several such tanks on the market but one may be built very simply and of a size conforming to the amount of eggs used. Care should be taken in constructing such a tank to be sure that the drain is installed at the proper height so that the water will be carried off at a level below the top of the cans of eggs so as to prevent any water getting into the cans.

After the eggs have been thawed, it is good practice to stir them thoroughly before incorporating them in the cake batter.

Frozen eggs should never be thawed by placing them in hot water or over the oven. Egg albumen begins to coagulate at 120°F. Coagulation means the whites will not whip up lightly and that the yolks will show up in the form of yellow specks throughout the cake.

Formulas calling for a given number of shell eggs or a given number of whites or yolks are essentially inaccurate because of the fact that eggs vary so much in size. However, for general work in the bakery, use the following basis for conversion:

1 pound Whole Egg	=	9-11 Shell Eggs
1 pound Egg White	=	15-17 Whites
1 pound Sugar-Yolk	=	22-24 Yolks

1. In what four forms are eggs commercially available?

2. What form of eggs is an important ingredient in most prepared cake mixes?

3. Name the most important function of eggs in cake making:

4. Why is a strong, firm-bodied white desirable for cake baking?

5. What does the egg yolk contribute to a cake?

6. What is the important consideration in buying shell eggs?

7. What is "candling" and for what purpose is it done?

8. Why should bakers buy their frozen eggs from a packer with a good reputation?

9. What are the four forms in which frozen eggs are generally available?

10. What are "fortified" eggs?

11. What are the advantages of high quality, spring-laid frozen eggs?

12. What are the two ways in which frozen eggs may be thawed prior to using?

13. Why should frozen eggs never be thawed by placing them in hot water or over the oven?

Leavening Agents

I.   DEFINITION

II. PURPOSES OF LEAVENING AGENTS

III. CLASSIFICATION

   A.   Chemical Leavener

      a.   Baking Powder
         1. Baking Powder, the "Soul of Cake"
         2. Baking Powder Defined
         3. Action of Baking Powder Explained
      b.   Cream of Tartar
      c.   Baking Soda
      d.   Ammonium Carbonate Type

   B.   Yeast

      a.   Compressed Yeast
      b.   Derivation of Word "Yeast"
      c.   The Function of Yeast in Bread Making
      d.   Characteristics of a Good Compressed Yeast
      e.   Active Dried Yeast

   C.   Leavening Achieved Mechanically

      a.   Leavening by Creaming
      b.   Leavening by Beaten Eggs

IV. STORAGE OF YEAST

   A.   Proper Temperature for Yeast Storage

   B.   Storage of Baking Powder

I. DEFINITION

Webster's definition for the word leaven "1. to raise. a. a substance (as yeast) used to produce fermentation in dough or liquid; esp. sour dough, b. a material (as baking powder) used to produce a gas that lightens dough or batter. 2. Something that modifies or lightens a mass or aggregate".

The two types of leavening most commonly used in baking today are: Organic (Yeast), and Chemical (Baking Powder–Baking Soda–Cream of Tartar–Ammonium Carbonate).

II. PURPOSES OF LEAVENING AGENTS

Importance of Leavening in Cakes or Breads

There are many factors that determine the quality of any baked product, but none is more important than the manner in which the batter or dough is raised or leavened, and the control of this leavening action.

If a cake batter or dough possessed no leavening power or, in other words, did not rise during baking, the resulting product would be dense, heavy and unpalatable. It would have little volume and would in no way resemble the light, porous and appetizing product which we know as "cake or bread". Proper leavening makes cakes more digestible.

III. CLASSIFICATION

Manner of Leavening and Cake Classification

There are several reasons why a cake batter or dough rises or becomes light during baking. The different types of cakes or breads have been roughly classified into three groups, each being characterized by the principal reason causing its leavening or rising. However, in a great number of cakes or breads, the leavening is the result of a combination of the actions explained in the following paragraphs.

A. Chemical Leavener

a. Baking Powder

In many of the cakes made today, such as loaf and layer cakes, wine cakes, various packaged cakes and cup cakes, as well as different kinds of cookies and biscuits, the principal leavening agent is baking powder. If it were not for baking powder, the many different varieties of delicious cakes produced today would not be possible. Therefore, the tremendous opportunity for the growth and development of the cake business today is in a measure due to the fact that baking powder in its present standardized form is available to the baker.

It must be remembered, however, that when converting a small handmade, household recipe to a large quantity batch for bake shop use, proportionate reductions should be made in the baking powder content to take care of the extra leavening brought about by creaming through mechanical means which is much more thorough than the hand method of creaming employed in the home.

1.   Baking Powder, the "Soul of the Cake"
While the other ingredients used can be considered the "body of the cake", it is the action of the baking powder that is mainly responsible for the conversion of the heavy mass of batter into a light, well-risen appetizing cake. As a matter of fact, the action of the baking powder influences many of the characteristics of the cake, such as symmetry, crust characteristics, volume, cell structure—which directly affect grain and texture, and to a very marked degree the eating and keeping quality of the cake. (See chart, p. 185)

2.   Baking Powder Defined
Baking powder is a leavening agent made up of a mixture of an acid or an acid-reacting salt, or combination of acid-reacting salts, with bicarbonate of soda. These substances are intimately mixed in balanced proportions, usually with a certain amount of specially dried starch which aids in keeping the powder in a dry condition and acts as a separator of the constituents of the powder until used.

3.   Action of Baking Powder Explained
In the presence of both heat and moisture, the acid-reacting salts act upon the bicarbonate of soda, releasing carbon dioxide gas. Part of this gas is absorbed by the liquid of the batter. The rest of this gas gradually pushes its way into the air cells (formed in creaming), helping them to expand and produce greater volume until the batter is finally "set" by the baking process. In this way the finished cake secures its light porous cell-like structure.

Baking powder distributed throughout the cake batter in the mixing process gradually loses its identity as the reaction producing the carbon dioxide gas proceeds. When this action is completed in the oven, the baking powder will have been used up, or destroyed, and in its place there are left residual substances, possibly together with traces of the original ingredients, which form a part of the cake itself. The character of this residue depends on the original composition of the powder used and may affect the flavor and color of the finished cake interior.

b.   Cream of Tartar
Cream of tartar is refined crude tartar which precipitates from grape wine during and after the process of fermentation. The pinkish crystallized sediments called lees, found at the bottom of the wine cask, and the pinkish crystalline substance called argols, that collects on the sides of the cask, are nothing but crude tartar.

The refining consists of a process of alternate decrystallizing of the crude tartar by cooking in boiling water, then allowing the resulting liquid to crystallize. The liquid is finally bleached to pure white and allowed to crystallize once more. As the liquid cools, a thin layer of white crystals forms on the surface. It is from this layer of white crystals that cream of tartar takes its name.

Cream of tartar is sold in powdered form. It has an acid taste and is used chiefly in the preparation of cream of tartar baking powder. For leavening purposes, two parts of cream of tartar are mixed with one part of baking soda.

c. Baking Soda

Baking soda (bicarbonate of sodium) is a side product in the manufacture of the common washing soda, also known as sal soda.

Sodium bicarbonate contains carbon and oxygen which form carbon dioxide gas. Hence, the reaction is similar whether a baking powder is used containing both the acid component and the sodium bicarbonate, or whether the sodium bicarbonate is added to a batter which has sufficient acidity in other ingredients to release the gas from the sodium bicarbonate.

An example of this is the addition of sodium bicarbonate to spice cakes containing molasses. The molasses is acid and is able to release the carbon dioxide gas from the added sodium bicarbonate.

d. Ammonium Carbonate Type

This type is a little different in its action. Like sodium bicarbonate, it also contains the constituents of carbon dioxide gas. Unlike the acid type, however, it does not require an acid or other substance to cause a reaction. Carbon dioxide gas is liberated from the ammonium carbonate by decomposition due to heat and moisture in the baking process. As it decomposes rapidly, it is used for the most part in cream puffs and cookies where a sudden expansion is desirable

B. Yeast

a. Compressed Yeast

Yeast is a microscopic one-celled plant belonging to the group known botanically as "fungi", which ordinarily multiplies by a process known as budding, and which under suitable conditions causes fermentation.

Each individual yeast plant is round or oval in shape and measures about 1/3600 inch in diameter. Each yeast cell is surrounded by a thin membrane of cellulose, and the interior of each cell is made up of finely granular protoplasm.

180

b. Derivation of Word Yeast

Our word "yeast" comes from the old Sanskrit "yas" meaning to seethe or boil, descriptive of its action in suitable sugary solutions from which it produces alcohol and carbon dioxide gas.

c. The Function of Yeast in Bread Making

Yeast raises and conditions the dough batch or, in other words, converts the inert, heavy mass of dough into a light, porous, elastic product that, when baked, is appetizing, easily digestible and nutritious. Yeast itself also adds definite food value to the loaf.

Without yeast, bread and other yeast-raised products as we know them today would not be possible.

Panary fermentation, brought about by the action of the yeast, represents the life process of the dough and upon this the creation of bread depends. Because of its fundamental and indispensable function in the production of leavened bread, yeast has been rightly termed the Soul of the Bread.

d. Characteristics of a Good Compressed Yeast
1. Purchased from a reliable manufacturer
2. Purity and uniformity are important
3. Hardness
4. Consistency, feel and fracture, firm and springy.
5. Taste and odor should be fresh and pleasant.
6. Appearance—light cream with a hue of yellowish or gray.

e. The Use of Active Dry Yeast
1. Determine amount of Active Dry Yeast required. If the formula is set up for Compressed Yeast, replace the Compressed Yeast with 40% as much Active Dry Yeast. On a weight basis, this will actually amount to 6.4 oz. (use 6½ oz.) of Active Dry Yeast to replace 1 lb. of Compressed Yeast, or 1 lb. of Active Dry Yeast for each 2½ lbs. of Compressed Yeast. To make calculation easier, see Active Dry Yeast replacement table.

2. Weigh out the exact amount of Active Dry Yeast required. Active Dry Yeast is convenient to use. Simply weigh out in the same manner as sugar, salt, or any other dry ingredient. Use a dry scoop because moisture affects the keeping quality of Active Dry Yeast.

3. Dissolve Active Dry Yeast in at least four times its weight of warm (not hot) water. Use part of the formula water for this purpose. The suggested amounts of water to use with various amounts of Active Dry Yeast will be found in the Replacement Table. In commercial practice, the temperature of the dissolving water may be from

90ºF. to 115ºF. However, for best results the temperature of the water in which this yeast is dissolved should be from 108º to 112ºF.

Temperatures lower than 90ºF. should not be used because as the water temperature is decreased, there is a tendency towards longer dissolving time, longer fermentation time, smaller loaf volume and poorer internal bread characteristics.

This is important when small amounts of Active Dry Yeast and water are used because, especially in cold weather or when cold utensils are used, the temperature of the water may fall below 90ºF. before the Active Dry Yeast is dissolved in it.

If at all possible, use a thermometer to determine dissolving water temperature. If Active Dry Yeast is dissolved in water below 90ºF. it will take longer to dissolve. At 140ºF. Active Dry Yeast, like Compressed Yeast, is "killed". In addition, using the same water temperature to dissolve the yeast for each dough will insure uniform fermentation activity.

If a thermometer is not available, the correct dissolving water temperature can be estimated fairly well with practice. The water should feel sightly warmer than body temperature.

4.   Dissolving Procedure—example: Where 1 lb. of Compressed Yeast is replaced by 6½ oz. of Active Dry Yeast.
  a.   Weigh 6½ oz. of Active Dry Yeast
  b.   Run 1 quart (about 2 pounds) of the formula water into pail or mixer. Water temperature should not be lower than 90ºF. (108º to 112ºF. for best results).
  c.   Add yeast to water IN A SLOW STREAM while stirring water so as to wet each yeast particle. (Yeast must be added SLOWLY. Add yeast to water. DO NOT ADD WATER TO YEAST.
  d.   Allow to soak 3 to 4 minutes while scaling other ingredients.
  e.   Stir until yeast is dissolved.
  f.   Use like Compressed Yeast. BE SURE TO SUBTRACT THE DISSOLVING WATER (in this example—2 pounds) FROM YOUR FORMULA WATER.

5.   Doughs made with Active Dry Yeast rather than Compressed Yeast will generally require from about 1¾ to 2 lbs. more water for each 1 lb. of Active Dry Yeast used. The exact amount of added water can be determined by observing the doughs made with Active Dry Yeast. This additional water, most of which compensates for the difference in moisture content between Active Dry Yeast and Com-

pressed Yeast, should be added to the sponge, or to the dough in the case of straight doughs.

6. If dough temperature is increased, dough time may be reduced slightly. The exact dough time can be determined by experience.

7. Dough mixing time may be decreased. The exact amount of reduction in time will vary according to shop conditions and can be determined by observing the first few doughs made with Active Dry Yeast.

STORAGE: Active Dry Yeast, like Compressed Yeast, is a form of plant life. Even though it is a dry product it is actually alive and should be stored in a cool dry place.

For best results, Active Dry Yeast for Bakers should be kept under refrigeration (below 45°F.) in a closed container.

If refrigeration is not available, Active Dry Yeast should be stored in a cool dry place in a closed container. Cover container tightly after each use. (Courtesy Fleischmann's Yeast Company).

C. Leavening Achieved Mechanically

a. Leavening by Creaming
When shortening and sugar are creamed together, we know that as the creaming process goes on, the mixture becomes lighter and occupies more volume. This is due to the fact that air is gradually being whipped into the mixture. Naturally, when this creamed mass is incorporated with the other ingredients in the cake mix, this air is locked up in the batter. When heated in the oven, these air cells, due to vaporization of moisture in the batter, expand and cause the cake to rise. The proper incorporation of air in the creaming process to a large extent controls the volume and structure of the finished cake. Old fashioned Pound Cake is an example of the class of cake in which this type of aeration, or leavening, is most prominent.

b. Leavening by Beaten Eggs
When eggs are beaten, we get a fluffy, foam-like mass, full of air. When this whipped mixture is incorporated into cake batter, the air which it contains is carried and held in the batter. The expansion of these air cells during baking causes the cake to rise, and to become light and porous.

Angel food, containing the beaten whites of eggs, and sponge cake, containing whole eggs previously whipped, are examples of the type of cake in which most of the leavening is secured in this way.

IV. STORAGE OF YEAST

A. Proper Temperature for Yeast Storage

Upon arrival at the bakery, the yeast should be placed in the refrigerator immediately. The temperature of the refrigerator for ideal yeast storage should be kept at about 45°F.

In the handling of yeast, it should never be forgotten that it is a living plant and, like all plants, it breathes in oxygen from the air and exhales carbon dioxide. This vital process of respiration is going on all of the time, proceeding very slowly indeed at low temperature, such as should be maintained in a refrigerator, and very rapidly at high temperature, such as is often met with in the bake shop in summer weather. As this vital process continues in the absence of food for the yeast, it gradually weakens. When the yeast is in a dough at 80°F., the case is different, for there is plenty of food in an ordinary dough for the requirements of the yeast. It is very important, therefore, that yeast should be kept cool to retard the respiration as much as possible until it is used.

In order to prevent any deterioration of yeast, extreme care is observed during manufacture and shipment, and the same precaution should be exercised by the baker so as to insure the greatest activity of his yeast in the dough batch.

B. Storage of Baking Powder

Practically all baking powders deteriorate with age. If bought in quantity and kept in storage for any length of time, they lose their strength, for they absorb some moisture and slowly give off gas. Furthermore, after storage for any considerable period of time, baking powder may become "caked" or lumpy, thus rendering it difficult to mix in uniformly with the flour.

In using a baking powder that has lost part of its original strength or uniformity through age, a baker is taking a dangerous and unnecessary gamble. It is certain that with such a baking powder, the quality of the finished cake will suffer noticeably and will not justify the expenditure made for the other ingredients that it contains. Therefore, the freshness of any baking powder can be considered as one of its foremost quality characteristics. Store baking powder in a cool dry place.

The action of baking powder may be pictured as follows:

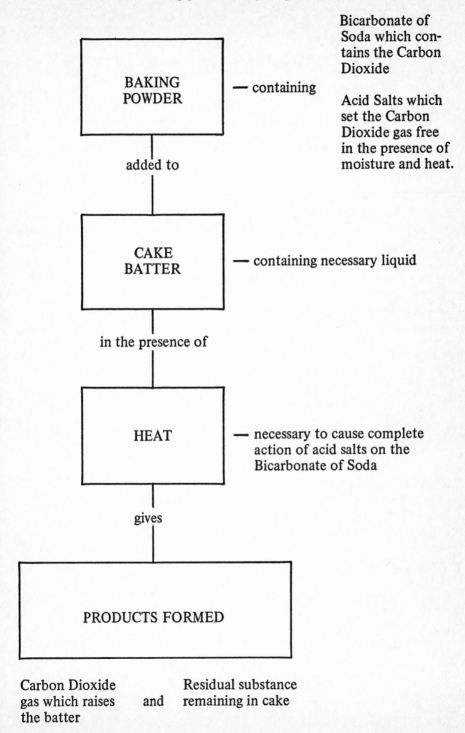

BAKING POWDER — containing

Bicarbonate of Soda which contains the Carbon Dioxide

Acid Salts which set the Carbon Dioxide gas free in the presence of moisture and heat.

added to

CAKE BATTER — containing necessary liquid

in the presence of

HEAT — necessary to cause complete action of acid salts on the Bicarbonate of Soda

gives

PRODUCTS FORMED

Carbon Dioxide gas which raises the batter   and   Residual substance remaining in cake

REVIEW

1. Name the two types of leavening agents most commonly used and give an example of each.

2. What is the importance of leavening in baking?

3. What is the principal leavening agent in cakes today?

4. What gas is liberated in the presence of moisture and heat?

5. What are the characteristics of a good compressed yeast?

6. What is the recommended procedure for storage of Active Dry Yeast?

7. Name two ways to achieve leavening mechanically.

8. Why do baking powders deteriorate with age?

9. Why is yeast called the "Soul of Bread?"

10. What should the temperature of the dissolving water for Active Dried Yeast be to yield the best results?

11. What is the effect of a lower dissolving water temperature than 90°F.?

12. If the dissolving water temperature reaches 140°F., what is the effect on the yeast?

Salt

I. SCIENTIFIC DEFINITION OF THE WORD SALT
   A. Common Salt or Sodium Chloride

II. SOURCE OF SALT

III. METHODS OF OBTAINING SALT FROM NATURAL SOURCES
   A. The Mining of Rock Salt
   B. Salt Obtained from Salt Brines
   C. Salt Secured from Ocean, Sea and Salt Lakes

IV. FUNCTION OF SALT IN BAKERY PRODUCTS
   A. Palatability Improved by Salt
   B. Effect of Salt on a Dough Fermentation
   C. Effect of Salt on Gluten-Texture and Grain of Product
   D. Effect of Salt on Crust Color

V. USE OF SALT IN BREAD DOUGH

VI. STORAGE OF SALT

I. SCIENTIFIC DEFINITION

From a strictly scientific standpoint, salts represent a certain class of substances or chemical compounds produced by the action of an alkali on an acid. In other words, if an acid and an alkali are mixed together they react with each other and form a new substance known as a salt.

A. Common Salt or Sodium Chloride
While there are hundreds of different kinds of salts which are well known to the chemist, the word "salt" in ordinary language refers to one particular salt, namely sodium chloride, which is the common salt universally used by every one as a mineral food.

This is the "salt" that is used in bakery products, salted butter, salted meats and a multitude of other foods, as well as for seasoning or flavoring in connection with practically every meal.

Salt is naturally present in many every day foods and has been recognized by man since very early times as an indispensable article of diet, necessary to sustain life and health.

II. SOURCE OF SALT

Nature has supplied us with salt in great abundance. It is found deposited in the earth in the form of salt beds and also dissolved in the water of the oceans, salt seas and lakes.

III. METHODS OF OBTAINING SALT FROM NATURAL SOURCES

A. The Mining of Rock Salt
In some sections of the United States and foreign countries, salt is "mined" from deposits of salt known as salt beds located below the surface of the earth, often at a depth of several hundred feet. Salt is secured from these mines in rather large irregular pieces and is known as rock salt, which is crushed, graded, and used as such, largely for the curing of hides, as food for cattle, and for many general industrial purposes.

Occasionally rock salt is obtained in a very pure state, but usually it contains small amounts of clay and other impurities when mined. To render this salt suitable for edible purposes, it is first necessary to put it through a careful process of purification in order to remove any objectionable substances that would impart an undesirable color or flavor to the salt.

B.   Salt Obtained from Salt Brines

A very large part of the salt used in this country is removed from the natural salt beds by first dissolving the salt in water so as to form a very strong salt solution known as brine. This is done by drilling down a six or eight inch hole until the salt deposit is reached. A pipe large enough to fit this hole is driven into the salt bed and inside of this another pipe about half as wide is driven down still further into the deposit of salt. Fresh water is forced into the outer pipe and soaks down through the salt bed, dissolving considerable amounts of the salt together with some impurities. The salt water thus produced is known as "artificial" brine and is pumped up through the inner pipe. In this way salt is removed from the underground deposit, without the necessity of constructing a mine. In certain localities, however, "natural" brine is obtained by merely boring into natural salt wells, which furnish a convenient source of salt.

In addition to common salt, both artificial and natural brines contain a small amount of other mineral substances, some of which impart an objectionable bitter or biting taste. The brine is evaporated in such a manner that these impurities may be separated out. Eventually, practically all of the water of the brine is driven off by evaporation, leaving the salt in crystallized form. This is then dried, sifted and graded.

In general, the size of the salt crystals secured can be more or less controlled by the method of evaporation employed. The salt sold for edible and baking purposes today is highly refined and free from objectionable substances. It is exceedingly pure and snow white in color.

C.   Salt Secured from Ocean, Sea and Lakes

In certain foreign countries, usually where the climate is dry and hot, as well as in California and Utah, salt is recovered from the water of oceans, salt seas and lakes. The salt water is first collected in large shallow open ponds or vats so that it will cover a large surface. The water is slowly evaporated by the heat of the sun until finally the salt crystallizes and separates out. Because of the use of the sun's rays for this purpose, salt thus produced is often called "Solar Salt". At various stages of the evaporation or concentration process, impurities separate out from the brine and are removed by passing the strong salt solution from one pond or vat to another. Finally, salt begins to crystallize out of the highly concentrated brine and continues to do so until practically all of the water has disappeared by evaporation. This salt is then collected, further purified, dried, crushed, sifted and graded.

IV. FUNCTION OF SALT IN BAKERY PRODUCTS

A. Palatability Improved by Salt

One of the most important functions of salt is its ability to improve the taste and flavor of all the foods in which it is used. Without salt in a dough batch, the resulting bread would be flat, insipid and lacking in flavor. The noticeable improvement in palatability brought about by the presence of salt is only partly due to the actual flavor of the salt itself. Improved palatability promotes the digestibility of food and because of this, salt enhances the nutritive value of bakery products. From the standpoint of palatability, the most pronounced effect of salt is its peculiar ability to intensify the flavor created in bread as a result of yeast action on the other dough batch ingredients that are blended together in the loaf. This results in bringing out that characteristic taste and flavor of good bread which is so eagerly sought for by the discriminating housewife. The best flavored bread is obtained by the maintenance of cool dough temperatures, the liberal use of salt and the use of sufficient yeast to bring about the necessary softening of the dough and the production of a light loaf in a reasonably short fermentation time.

B. Effect of Salt on Dough Fermentation

It may be well to repeat briefly that while the action of yeast is responsible for the fermentation of the dough, it is the salt present that helps to govern or control this activity.

Although the amount of salt used in bread doughs tends to lessen the rate of yeast activity, its ability to prevent the development of any objectionable bacterial action or wild types of fermentation is much more pronounced. In this way, salt, when used in proper amounts, aids in checking the development of any undesirable or excessive acidity in the dough batch.

Thus, it is seen that salt performs a very valuable function in bread making. It governs the important changes involved in the conditioning of the dough, affords protection against any undesirable action in the dough and, in general, assists in the promotion of a normal, healthy panary fermentation process which is necessary in order to secure a finished product of high quality.

C. Effect of Salt on Gluten—Texture and Grain of Product

Salt has a binding or strengthening effect on gluten and thereby adds strength to any flour. The additional firmness imparted to the gluten by the salt enables it to hold water and the gas, carbon dioxide, more efficiently and to expand nicely without tearing. This results in a finer grained loaf of superior texture. While salt has no direct bleaching effect on bread, the fine grain and thin cell walls produced give the crumb of the loaf a whiter appearance.

D. Effect of Salt on Crust Color

By lessening the destruction of sugar in the dough, salt indirectly assists in the promotion of a deeper crust color.

V. USE OF SALT IN A BREAD DOUGH

Because of the very important action of salt in bread making, it is essential that liberal quantities of refined high grade salt should be used. The average amount is about 1¾ to 2¼ pounds to every hundred pounds of flour. Some authorities recommend that the amount of salt used should be based on the actual quantity of water employed in making up the dough batch, namely about ½ ounce to every pound of water.

The upper limit of the quantity of salt that can be successfully used is usually governed by the taste of the resulting loaf. During the hot summer months, many bakers find it of advantage to use slightly more salt than in the winter, as a safeguard against the development of any undesirable changes in character of the dough fermentation.

In bread made by the Sponge-and-Dough Method, it is advantageous to use a small portion of the salt in the sponge part where it is valuable in strengthening the gluten.

Salt is usually first dissolved in the bulk of the water together with the sugar and malt syrup before mixing into the dough. It is very important to see that the salt is not dissolved in that portion of the water in which the yeast is dissolved before incorporation into the dough batch.

VI. STORAGE OF SALT

Salt is very stable and does not spoil under ordinary conditions. However, it may have a slight tendency to absorb moisture and to get somewhat lumpy or hard. Therefore, it is advisable to store it in a clean, cool, dry place. Inasmuch as salt can absorb odors, the storage room should be quite free from any odors that might be taken up and carried by the salt.

REVIEW

1. How are salts produced?

2. What is the chemical name of common salt?

3. Name two sources of salt.

4. How does salt improve the palatability of bread?

5. What is the effect of salt on dough fermentation?

6. What is the effect of salt on gluten?

7. Why does salt give a whiter appearance to the crumb of the loaf?

8. How does the use of salt help to promote a deeper crust color?

9. What is the average amount of salt that should be used for every 100 lbs. of flour?

10. Why should salt be stored in a clean, cool, dry place?

Layouts for Bake Shops

SIZE 50x50   # Plan 1   SQ. FT. 2,500

Approx. Sq. Ft. of Equipment 830.09

Approx. Floor Space Used by Equipment 30.11%

Investigation indicates that the floor plan illustrated in this layout is representative of one type found in many places throughout the country.

This layout is designed to give ideas for efficient flow of production to the large number of bakers who are planning on remodelling or building shops.

Each baker must consider his own production problems and then select the equipment he judges most suitable to his needs. Only the most essential shop equipment is shown in the layout. Dressing rooms, basements, etc., have been omitted to permit concentration on production flow.

Good sanitation has been a major consideration. Tile walls and smooth surface floor and equipment have been indicated wherever possible to make cleaning easy.

Remember that an immaculate shop with good rodent-proof foundations not only complies with sanitation laws, but also increases efficiency and raises the quality of finished baked goods.

Practical application of the layout suggestions will result in the saving of many steps—the elimination of needless criss-crossing and back-tracking —in short—Production Efficiency.

Follow the flow of production ➡

① **Ingredient Storage** ➡ The double outside door is conveniently located for the delivery of bulky bakery material. The door to the icing and finishing department (7) serves a dual purpose—gives quick, easy access from this department to the ingredients, and also permits used pans to be easily brought to the pan washing machine. Stairs to the basement are out of the line of production, but are conveniently located near the double outside door.

② **Scaling** ➡ Actual production starts with scaling. Therefore, the ingredient bench where the scaling operation is performed is conveniently located near ingredient storage.

③ **Mixing** ➡ For convenience, mixers are located close to the bench where ingredients are scaled and are in line with a large sink and gas stove.

④ **Make-up** ➡ The make-up section is located between the mixers and ovens. It includes one combination fermentation work bench and one large work table which give sufficient working surface to handle yeast-raised products, cakes and pastries.

⑤ **Proofing and Retarding** ➡ Closely allied to the make-up section, the 4-door refrigerator, used primarily for retarding, and the proof box have clear paths to the oven.

⑥ **Baking** ➡ Plenty of baking space is provided. One oven, used primarily for baking yeast-raised products, is located in close proximity to the proof box and refrigerator, which is used for retarding. The other two ovens are generally used for cake, pastry, etc., and are convenient to the make-up section. The location of all ovens permits easy access to the icing and finishing department.

⑦ **Icing and Finishing** ➡ In this department more than adequate rack space is provided. A sink, refrigerator, gas stove and tables make a finely equipped icing and finishing department close to the entrance to the store.

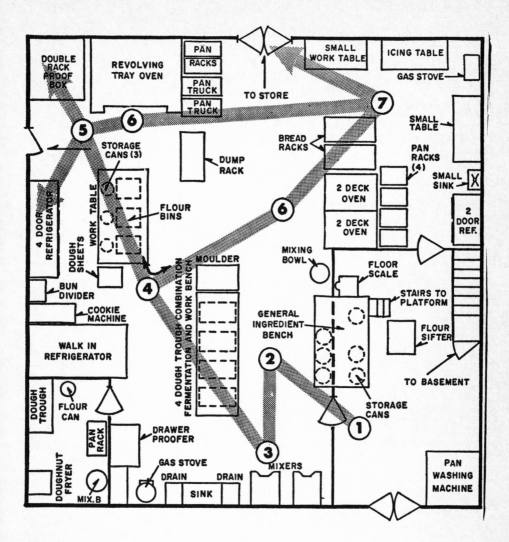

PLAN NO. 1

SHOP EQUIPMENT	APPROXIMATE SIZE		APPROX. TOTAL
	LENGTH	WIDTH	SQUARE FEET
Revolving Tray Oven	10'3"	x 7'10½"	80.71
2 Two-Deck Ovens	4'1½"	x 6'	49.50
2-Rack Proof Box	5'10½"	x 5'6"	32.31
2 Mixers	4'	x 2'6"	20.00
Combination Fermentation & Work Bench	14'	x 5'	70.00
Work Table	10'	x 5'6"	55.00
2 Small Work Tables	7'	x 3'	42.00
Icing Table	8'	x 3'	24.00
Dough Trough Bench	6'	x 2'7½"	15.75
Walk-in Refrigerator	10'1½"	x 5'	50.62
4-Door Refrigerator	10'3"	x 3'	30.75
2-Door Refrigerator	5'6"	x 3'1½"	17.18
Moulder	5'10½"	x 3'	17.62
Cookie Machine	6'	x 2'	12.00
Drawer Proofer	4'6"	x 3'3"	14.62
Dough Sheeter	2'10½"	x 2'3"	6.46
Pan Washing Machine	6'3"	x 5'9"	35.93
Roll & Bun Divider	2'	x 1'9"	3.50
Flour Sifter	3'7½"	x 3'	10.87
7 Pan Racks	3'1½"	x 2'	43.75
2 Pan Trucks	4'6"	x 2'1½"	19.12
2 Bread Racks	5'9"	x 2'4½"	27.30
Dump Rack	5'9"	x 3'	17.25
Doughnut Fryer	2'7½"	x 2'3"	5.90
Gas Stove (Hot Plate)	2'6"	x 1'3"	3.12
Gas Stove	2'3"	x 2'	4.50
General Ingredient Bench	10'4½"	x 5'10½"	60.95
Storage Cabinet	3'7½"	x 2'6"	9.06
4 Dough Troughs	4'4½"	x 2'3"	39.36*
Small Sink	2'	x 1'7½"	3.25
Sink & 2 Drain Boards	8'6"	x 2'	17.00
2 Mixing Bowls and Stands	2'7½"	x 2'7½"	13.78
Floor Scale	3'6"	x 2'4½"	8.31
9 Storage Cans	1'9" Dia.		21.60*
1 Storage Can	1'9" Dia.		2.40
3 Flour Bins	2'4½"	x 1'10½"	13.35*
Stairs (Ingredient Bench)	2'7½"	x 2'1½"	5.58
		GROSS TOTAL	904.40
*LESS EQUIPMENT UNDER TABLES AND BENCHES			74.31
		NET TOTAL	830.09

Plan 2

SIZE 30x51 SQ. FT. 1,530

Approx. Sq. Ft. of Equipment 491.95

Approx. Floor Space Used by Equipment 32.15%

Investigation indicates that the floor plan illustrated in this layout is representative of one type found in many places throughout the country.

This layout is designed to give ideas for efficient flow of production to the large number of bakers who are planning on remodelling or building shops.

Each baker must consider his own production problems and then select the equipment he judges most suitable to his needs. Only the most essential shop equipment is shown in the layout. Dressing rooms, basements, etc., have been omitted to permit concentration on production flow.

Good sanitation has been a major consideration. Tile walls and smooth surface floor and equipment have been indicated wherever possible to make cleaning easy.

Remember that an immaculate shop with good rodent-proof foundations not only complies with sanitation laws, but also increases efficiency and raises the quality of finished baked goods.

Practical application of the layout suggestions will result in the saving of many steps—the elimination of needless criss-crossing and back-tracking —in short—Production Efficiency.

Follow the flow of production ➡

(1) Ingredient Storage and Scaling ➡ In order to achieve a smooth and logical flow of production, the operation in this plan commences at the front of the production shop. Ingredients are stored beneath the large and small work tables as well as in storage cans. The ingredients are scaled on the small work table, which has built-in storage compartments.

(2) Mixing ➡ The mixer is located near the scaling operation and within easy reach of the large work table and dough troughs. The sink is next to the mixer.

(3) Make-up and Retarding ➡ In the make-up section the large work table with dough troughs beneath is in the center of the production shop. It is thus possible for bakers to work at either side and at one end of this table. At the other end, the dough sheeter and bun divider can be conveniently operated. The 4-door refrigerator, used for retarding, is within easy reach and both have a clear path to the proof box and oven.

(4) Proofing and Baking ➡ Both the oven and proof box are closely allied to the work tables. The built-in feature of the oven keeps heat and fumes from the production shop. Clear access is provided to the icing and finishing department

(5) Icing and Finishing ➡ The icing and finishing department has adequate rack space and plenty of table working surface. Equipped with a small sink and icing stove, this department is designed for efficiency. The large opening leading to the store permits the passage of racks of finished products.

FLOOR PLAN
NO. 2
30' X 51'
0   1   2   3   4
FEET

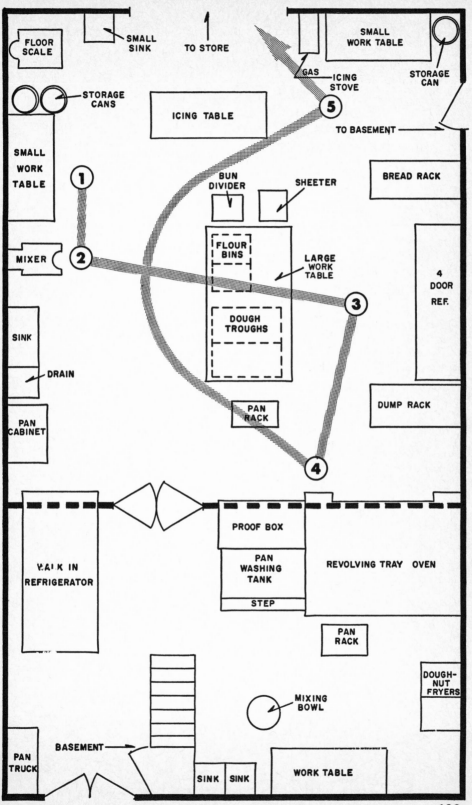

SHOP EQUIPMENT	APPROXIMATE SIZE LENGTH		WIDTH	APPROX. TOTAL SQUARE FEET
Revolving Tray Oven	10'3"	x	7'10½"	80.71
Proof Box	5'10½"	x	2'9"	16.15
Mixer	4'	x	2'6"	10.00
Large Work Table	10'	x	5'6"	55.00
3 Small Work Tables	7'	x	3'	63.00
Icing Table	8'	x	3'	24.00
Walk-in Refrigerator	10'1½"	x	5'	50.62
4-Door Refrigerator	10'3"	x	3'	30.75
Sheeter	2'10½"	x	2'3"	6.46
Bun Divider	2'	x	1'9"	3.50
Pan Washing Tank & Steps	5'10½"	x	4'7½"	27.17
Sink & Drain Board	6'6"	x	2'	13.00
Small Sink	2'	x	1'7½"	3.25
Double Sink	4'6"	x	2'	9.00
2 Doughnut Fryers	2'7½"	x	2'3"	11.80
Gas & Icing Stove	2'6"	x	1'3"	3.12
Floor Scale	3'6"	x	2'4½"	8.31
3 Storage Cans	1'9" Dia.			7.20
2 Flour Bins	2'4½"	x	1'10½"	8.90*
2 Dough Troughs	4'4½"	x	2'3"	19.68*
2 Pan Racks	3'1½"	x	2'	12.50
Bread Rack	5'9"	x	2'4½"	13.65
Pan Truck	4'6"	x	2'1½"	9.56
Pan Cabinet	3'7½"	x	2'6"	9.06
Dump Rack	5'9"	x	3'	17.25
Mixing Bowl & Stand	2'7½"	x	2'7½"	6.89

GROSS TOTAL 520.53

*LESS EQUIPMENT UNDER TABLES AND BENCHES 28.58

NET TOTAL 491.95

Plan 3

Approx. Sq. Ft. of Equipment 333.51

Approx. Floor Space Used by Equipment 41.68%

Investigation indicates that the floor plan illustrated in this layout is representative of one type found in many places throughout the country.

This layout is designed to give ideas for efficient flow of production to the large number of bakers who are planning on remodelling or building shops.

Each baker must consider his own production problems and then select the equipment he judges most suitable to his needs. Only the most essential shop equipment is shown in the layout. Dressing rooms, basements, etc., have been omitted to permit concentration on production flow.

Good sanitation has been a major consideration. Tile walls and smooth surface floor and equipment have been indicated wherever possible to make cleaning easy.

Remember that an immaculate shop with good rodent-proof foundations not only complies with sanitation laws, but also increases efficiency and raises the quality of finished baked goods.

Practical application of the layout suggestions will result in the saving of many steps—the elimination of needless criss-crossing and back-tracking —in short—Production Efficiency.

Follow the flow of production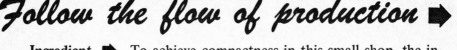

(1) Ingredient Storage and Scaling ➡ To achieve compactness in this small shop, the ingredients are stored beneath both the large and small work tables. Ingredients are generally scaled on the small table and, therefore, it is located next to the mixer.

(2) Mixing ➡ For convenience, the mixer is located close to the scaling operation and also close to both the work tables and the dough trough bench. The gas stove is conveniently located in the corner near the mixer.

(3) Make-up and Retarding ➡ To eliminate waste motion, the large work table is centrally located. The refrigerator used for retarding and storage is next to the proof box and handy to the large work table.

(4) Proofing ➡ The proof box is located so that there is a clear passage to the large work table, refrigerator and oven.

(5) Baking ➡ The cross-shop position of the oven enables the baker to observe baking while performing other duties.

(6) Icing and Finishing ➡ The compact icing and finishing department has plenty of work space, ample room for the icing table, a small sink and movable racks. It is ideally situated close to the double doors leading to the store.

FLOOR PLAN NO.3
20' X 40'

0 1 2 3 4
FEET

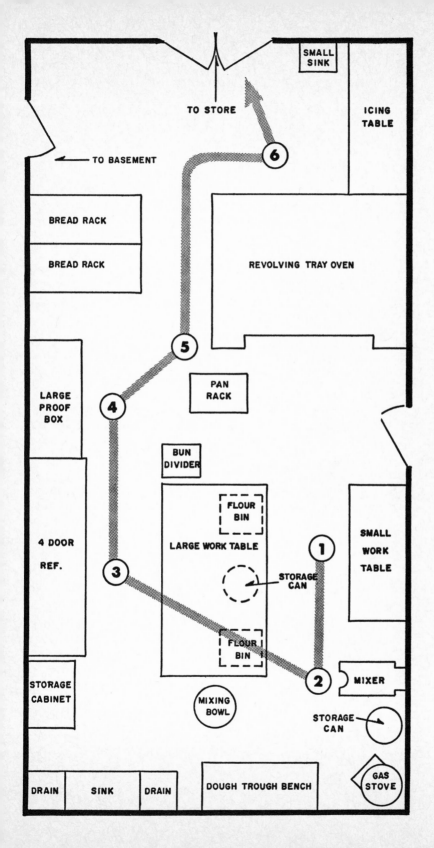

SMALL SINK

ICING TABLE

TO STORE

TO BASEMENT

BREAD RACK

BREAD RACK

REVOLVING TRAY OVEN

LARGE PROOF BOX

PAN RACK

BUN DIVIDER

4 DOOR REF.

FLOUR BIN

LARGE WORK TABLE

STORAGE CAN

SMALL WORK TABLE

FLOUR BIN

MIXER

STORAGE CABINET

MIXING BOWL

STORAGE CAN

DRAIN

SINK

DRAIN

DOUGH TROUGH BENCH

GAS STOVE

PLAN NO. 3

SHOP EQUIPMENT	APPROXIMATE SIZE LENGTH		WIDTH	APPROX. TOTAL SQUARE FEET
Revolving Tray Oven	10'3"	x	7'10½"	80.71
Large Proof Box	5'10½"	x	2'9"	16.15
Mixer	4'	x	2'6"	10.00
Large Work Table	10'	x	5'6"	55.00
Small Work Table	7'	x	3'	21.00
Icing Table	8'	x	3'	24.00
Dough Trough Bench	6'	x	2'7½"	15.75
4-Door Refrigerator	10'3"	x	3'	30.75
Bun Divider	2'	x	1'9"	3.50
Sink & 2 Drain Boards	8'6"	x	2'	17.00
Small Sink	2'	x	1'7½"	3.25
Gas Stove	2'3"	x	2'	4.50
1 Storage Can	1'9" Dia.			2.40*
1 Storage Can	1'9" Dia.			2.40
2 Flour Bins	2'4½"	x	1'10½"	8.90*
Pan Rack	3'1½"	x	2'	6.25
2 Bread Racks	5'9"	x	2'4½"	27.30
Storage Cabinet	3'7½"	x	2'6"	9.06
Mixing Bowl & Stand	2'7½"	x	2'7½"	6.89

GROSS TOTAL   344.81

*LESS EQUIPMENT UNDER TABLES AND BENCHES   11.30

NET TOTAL   333.51

Plan 4

Approx. Sq. Ft. of Equipment 204.84

Approx. Floor Space Used by Equipment 28.45%

Investigation indicates that the floor plan illustrated in this layout is representative of one type found in many places throughout the country.

This layout is designed to give ideas for efficient flow of production to the large number of bakers who are planning on remodelling or building shops.

Each baker must consider his own production problems and then select the equipment he judges most suitable to his needs. Only the most essential shop equipment is shown in the layout. Dressing rooms, basements, etc., have been omitted to permit concentration on production flow.

Good sanitation has been a major consideration. Tile walls and smooth surface floor and equipment have been indicated wherever possible to make cleaning easy.

Remember that an immaculate shop with good rodent-proof foundations not only complies with sanitation laws, but also increases efficiency and raises the quality of finished baked goods.

Practical application of the layout suggestions will result in the saving of many steps—the elimination of needless criss-crossing and back-tracking —in short—Production Efficiency.

Follow the flow of production ➡

① Ingredient Storage and Scaling ➡ Small ingredients are stored in built-in compartments beneath the work tables—flour storage bins are located next to the mixer. Ingredients are scaled on the centrally located work tables.

② Mixing ➡ The mixer is located close to the combination ingredient scaling and work tables. It is convenient to the large double sink.

③ Make-up and Retarding ➡ The make-up operations, like the scaling, is carried out on the centrally located work tables and also on the dough trough bench. The refrigerator is located near the work tables, for in such a small shop, it must serve a dual purpose,—as a retarder and for the storage of ingredients.

④ Proofing and Baking ➡ The proof box and double deck oven are conveniently located near the central work tables.

⑤ Icing and Finishing ➡ Baked products are iced and finished on the central work tables. The finished products are then stored on racks at the store entrance or taken directly to the store.

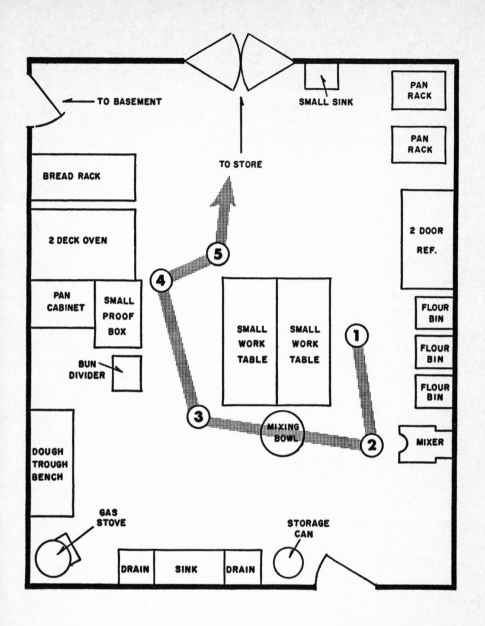

TO BASEMENT

SMALL SINK

PAN RACK

PAN RACK

BREAD RACK

2 DECK OVEN

TO STORE

2 DOOR REF.

PAN CABINET

SMALL PROOF BOX

FLOUR BIN

FLOUR BIN

FLOUR BIN

BUN DIVIDER

SMALL WORK TABLE

SMALL WORK TABLE

①

DOUGH TROUGH BENCH

④

⑤

③

MIXING BOWL

②

MIXER

GAS STOVE

STORAGE CAN

DRAIN

SINK

DRAIN

FLOOR PLAN NO. 4
24' X 30'

0 1 2 3 4
FEET

PLAN NO. 4

SHOP EQUIPMENT	APPROXIMATE SIZE		APPROX. TOTAL SQUARE FEET
	LENGTH	WIDTH	
2-Deck Oven	4'1½"	x 6'	24.75
Small Proof Box	3'7½"	x 2'6"	9.06
Mixer	4'	x 2'6"	10.00
2 Small Work Tables	7'	x 3'	42.00
Dough Trough Bench	6'	x 2'7½"	15.75
2-Door Refrigerator	5'6"	x 3'1½"	17.18
Bun Divider	2'	x 1'9	3.50
Gas Stove	2'3"	x 2'	4.50
Sink & 2 Drain Boards	8'6"	x 2'	17.00
Small Sink	2'	x 1'7½"	3.25
Storage Can	1'9" Dia.		2.40
3 Flour Bins	2'4½"	x 1'10½"	13.35
Bread Rack	5'9"	x 2'4½"	13.65
2 Pan Racks	3'1½"	x 2'	12.50
Pan Cabinet	3'7½"	x 2'6"	9.06
Mixing Bowl & Stand	2'7½"	x 2'7½"	6.89

NET TOTAL   204.84

INDEX

212